Book I

THE TEACHER

In Their Shoes - The Teacher (Book 1)

Written by Andrew Mackay with Joy Attwood

Edited by Drew Cullingham

Cover design and illustrations by Kreacher

ChromeValleyBooks.com

ISBN-10: 1539463451
ISBN-13: 978-1539463450
Copyright © 2016 - Chrome Valley Books

Chapters

1

In Their Shoes:
Rachel Weir (A Teacher)

It was 8:02am on a bright Monday May morning. I was leaning against my Gold Ford Fiesta in the smaller of two car parks at Maxwell Gooder's Comprehensive School in Fingeringham, Wiltshire.

The school is named after celebrated industrial pioneer Maxwell Gooder (1820 - 1851) who, at the relatively young age of thirty years old, managed to castrate himself whilst trying to open a tin of biscuits. His obituary at Fingeringham's department of births, marriages and deaths recorded the cause of death as "*capitulating to faggotry*".

The drive from London was an easy one; the motorway was relatively empty on my journey here, and it wasn't until I arrived at Fingeringham that my navigation app gave up the ghost completely due to the lack of a useful (let alone 4G) signal.

I eventually found Maxwell Gooder's itself thanks to a couple of year seven students making their way to school. The girls had seen me traverse the main grounds of the building in my car a number of times, and went on to make it clear that they had become increasingly concerned for their safety.

As I stood in the warm May morning sun the threat of

much severer heat hung above the surrounding foliage. I'd been waiting for nearly thirty minutes by this point and my anxiety was turning to impatience. The teacher I was waiting for was Ms Rachel Weir - Maxwell Gooder's sole teacher of English and Business Studies.

The larger car park attached to the school building screamed "Hey, I'm diligent and care about my work, and don't mind you seeing me arriving early!" The same cannot be said for the car park I was waiting in; a meek pretender, probably reserved for events (such as parents evenings) whose inhabitants must surely only take advantage of due to its inauspicious setting.

As I pondered all this a red Volvo trumped into the mouth of the car park, splashing through the very same puddle I traversed thirty minutes ago. The car rolled up directly opposite my own and jolts to a stop. I peered over. I could make out the shape of a lady sitting inside, wrestling with her seatbelt as the faint sound of pop music - Sax by Fleur East - blared from the crevice of the slightly open driver's window.

The music stopped.

Stepping forward cautiously to glean a better view, I saw the side of the red Volvo. The door flung open to its fullest, sending it crashing back into the knee of the occupier. One could instinctively feel - even mere yards away - that this might not have been the best start to someone's day. A strapped boot kicked the door open again and out came a woman, seemingly in a world of haste trying to exit her car - only for her seatbelt to constrict said action and yank her back to her seat.

That was two pratfalls already. Something told me this is Rachel. I hurried over and offered my assistance.

'Excuse me,' I said, trying to minimise any embarrassment my arrival may be causing. 'Are you Rachel Weir?'

'Ugh, I just wanna go home.' Ms. Weir shoved a clump of papers into my chest, which I quickly caught as she unfastened her seatbelt and stood vertically for the first time with a small grimace of victory sprawled across her face.

Her face was at once sullen - somewhat pale, indicating a night spent possibly not in the way she'd have liked. Indeed, this proved to be true as she took my shoulder, squeezed the veins solidly shut, and doubled over herself, hanging her face in the bushes. She then vomited a dark yellow substance onto the floor and heaved, wiping the drool away from her mouth with her sleeve.

An awkward pause underscored our initiation.

Rachel took a moment to tilt her head up toward the hazy, warm sun. 'Ugh, God. I feel like I've just sucked a thousand dicks,' Rachel burped, 'aww shit. I'm sorry I completely forgot it was today.'

'Oh that's quite all right. In fact, it's probably better you pretend I'm not here,' I said, as I saw her checking her watch. Her eyes widened, as if she'd received bad news.

'Shit!' Rachel swiped the papers she had handed me from my arms and began hot-stepping it toward the direction of the school. I traipsed after her.

'Is everything okay?'

'Oh. I'm sure it is for everyone else. But for me? Uh, not likely. I've got ten minutes before the morning meeting and I need my morning coffee,' she continued, glancing at me as I caught up to her, 'or else people die. And the majority of people in schools are children. SMT take a very dim view of children dying at the workplace,' Rachel tailed off under her breath, having made her point.

I smiled so as not to agitate this already-hassled woman. In this line of work it's better to play the distant dummy and just nod and agree. I extended my right hand for her to shake as we approach the school entrance.

'Joy Attwood.'

'Rachel Weir, good to meet you at last,' she said as doggedly determined to walk as if she's in The West Wing. 'You'll need to sign in. Did you bring your DBS certificate with you?'

'Uh, no?' I suddenly got worried. 'I wasn't told I needed one?'

We approached the main glass door of the entrance. Rachel clasped the handle with her hand. 'That's okay, we'll just do what we normally do,' she said as she yanked the door open. 'We'll lie.'

The entrance to the school was (and presumably still is) large and the walls were high as you'd expect in any modern comprehensive secondary, there were displays of art from students. A colourful Picasso-esque painting of something and a few large canvas art prints of Laurel & Hardy and well-known artists of the twentieth century adorned the walls. And of course, like any decent and fully functioning school - a reception desk. This one resembled the grey, static monotony of a National Rail station. When the teller behind the window spoke that particular description was perfected.

'Good morning ladies!' said the receptionist, with a conversational drawl that suggested she'd not fully completed the birthing process fifty-two years ago.

'Gail, this is Jane Altwood—'

'—actually it's Joy.'

'Sorry, Joy Alterwood?'

'No, my surname is Attwood.'

'What?'

The receptionist held up her hand and shook her head. 'No, no, start again for me. You are Joy Alterwood?' she asked. Rachel examined her wristwatch in a huff, eager to make a move.

'No. It's Attwood, actually,' I said.

'Can I see your DBS certificate, please.'

'I don't have it with me, I'm afraid,' I replied.

'Okay,' the receptionist said. She looked at Rachel. 'Your visitor must be escorted at all times, Ms Weir.'

'Yes, yes,' Rachel snapped. 'Fine, whatever.'

The receptionist adjusted her spectacles and wrote down my full name on the visitor slip. She folded it up and inserted it into a blue lanyard. I thanked her duly and, as I retrieved the item, noticed my visitor's badge gave a deceptively different idea of the person it now announced; *Joyce Altwild*.

Rachel scanned the pass and tittered to herself as she read it. 'Don't worry,' she said as she tapped my shoulder, indicating the need to leave. 'It'll do, no-one cares. We've got five minutes.'

We marched into the school proper.

As Rachel and I emerged through the double doors, we were greeted with a giant, circular playground with hulking two-storey buildings either side of it. At first glance, you'd be forgiven for thinking that whoever designed the Roman Colosseum had a nightmare one night and dreamt this monstrosity up. Every few feet had five-foot high rectangular windows, which possessed the visual vibe of two screaming giants on permanent "rage mode", enacting a pincer movement of punishment on the screaming children below during playtime.

8:18am. A few students in their blue and black uniforms were straddling the benches, listening to music on their iPods (or whatever those devices are). They were difficult to see from this distance.

We circumvented two oncoming boys as we marched toward the stairs, the walls of which were painted pink. The two boys - no older than thirteen - gawped at my legs.

'Nice Jeans, Miss!' one of them giggled. They smiled at me as we move past them. I smiled back as Rachel and I ascend the stairs.

The handrails were surprisingly clean.

'Okay, nearly there. Just need to dump my papers on the desk, switch on the computer and get the coffee going,' Rachel revealed as we reached the first floor English corridor.

It was a long, long corridor. The sunlight illuminated the door of room 814. A sneak preview of what was in store was offered in the form of a circular window that promised a typical, if fairly lengthy, classroom behind it.

As Rachel fumbled for her keys - loudly - I noticed that the door had a landscape A4 laminated sticker on it. 'Ms R. Weir'. Rachel saw me clocking the name tag and smiled as she inserted her key and opened the door.

'Yeah. No expense spent here, my friend.'

Rachel leapt into the room as if the corridor were suddenly ablaze. I sauntered in behind her, looking around at Rachel's professional home - the room was long in width and short in depth. Split into two halves. The half we were in had a white board and computer screen and student chairs and tables. The other half, in darkness for the moment, contained four banks of individual computers and monitors.

'So, this is your classroom, Rachel? Very nice!'

Rachel sifted through her papers with one hand, and pressed the "on" switch on her computer with the other. 'Yeah, this is chez Weir. Oh, and by the way, when the kids are within earshot, I'm Ms. Weir, not Rachel.'

'Can I ask why that is?'

'So that the kids get used to formality,' said Rachel, as her computer "ping'ed to life. She opened the top drawer of her computer desk, fumbling for something.

'We can't very well have them calling us Rachel and Brian and so on, can we? That'd undermine our authority. A-ha!' Rachel smiled, took out a coffee sachet and slammed the drawer shut with her knee.

On the screen, a crude smiley face made up of random letters of the alphabet blinked back at us. Above it read Electronic Juvenile Information Terminal accompanied by a flashing log-in screen below. 'Ugh, hello to you too,' Rachel said to the machine. 'This thing never works. Right, let's get the kettle on pronto.'

Rachel made for the door - the reality of the day started

to kick in. 'There's no way I'm sitting through that morning meeting without my ritual caffeine insemination,' she snapped to herself as she walked past me.

2

Only Six Thousand, Five Hundred and Forty Minutes Until the Weekend Starts

The staffroom was like an IT geek's haven - full of broken computers and staff desks arranged in ways that would send an obsessive compulsive over the edge. As we walked in I saw a man with glasses busily working at one of the computers. There was a man with white overalls in the corner of the room, and an older gentleman in a shirt and tie talking to a younger woman at her laptop who peered up at Rachel, and then to me.

'You're late, Raych. Road accident?'

'Hey everyone, hey Gemma,' Rachel said, as she hit the switch on the kettle on top of the cupboard. Everyone nodded back and smiled as Rachel waved the sachet around in her hand and tore off the top. 'Everyone, this is Jane—'

'It's Joy, actually.'

'Joy. Sorry. She's following me around today for a book!'

Everyone smiled at me.

'Heavy night last night, Gemma. If you don't believe me, ask the bush outside!'

This was surprising in some ways. As a journalist, I'd been led to believe that teachers were walking baggages of inner turmoil who scowled at strangers trying to espouse the virtues of their profession to the great unwashed public. I found the air in this particular staff room to be fairly relaxed.

Rachel walked over to Gemma and the older gentleman as I began my enquiries.

'So this is the staff room?'

I followed Rachel further into the room. 'How many staff members actually share this room?'

'Oh, there are probably about twelve staff rooms across the entire school. This is mainly for business and English. IT services are also based here, as this is the most common area of the school.'

'And how many staff and students are there at this school?'

'There's one thousand students, give or take, year seven through sixth form,' Rachel said as she turned to Gemma. 'And how many staff?'

'There's about eighty teaching staff and—' Gemma's eyes seared around the wall chart hanging above her head. '—I think about thirty non-teaching.'

'Sorry, Joy. This is Gemma. She's Head of Computer Science.'

'Hi, nice to meet you.'

Gemma and I shook hands. Her handshake was rather light, which was to be expected from a girl with such a small frame.

'How long have you worked here, Gemma?'

'About a year and half,' she replied. 'Yeah, only four more days now till half term! Oh, and this is Gareth.' She walked me over to a sensationally attractive young man with spectacles. 'He looks after the E-JIT.'

'The Eejit?'

Gareth chuckled. 'Yeah, that's me,' he said. He thumped the side of the machine and pretended that the action had made it spring to life. He clearly wasn't too fond of the new device.

'So this piece of crap is called the E-JIT. It's the local network for the school's system. It carries all the information on students, records, registers and that kind of thing. Here, have a look.' Gareth rolled himself to the side of his desk - revealing that he was in a wheelchair. 'This is the main log-in screen.'

It was exactly the same log-in as the one I saw on Rachel's monitor.

'And if I log in, voila!' Gareth types in his password and hits enter. Incorrect password. He types it again. Same thing. 'Bollocks. It's not recognising my password!' Gareth forgets I'm watching and immediately goes for his mobile phone.

Rachel rapped me on the shoulder as Gemma stood up alongside her male colleague (whom I was yet to meet formally). 'It's 8:20, we'd better get down now,' says Gemma, making her way to the door.

The kettle finally blew its last whistle as we moved past it. Rachel shot it a look and then carried on the evil glare, stubbornly. 'Well, I guess it'll have to wait till after the meeting.'

8:25am. Rachel, Gemma and I slowly made our way to three available plastic seats that lined the back wall. There was probably around sixty chairs in this cramped room, but what really caught my attention were the banks of chairs facing away from each other. The adults sitting on the chairs were clearly teachers of some description. There was a man in a shirt and tie half asleep by the water fountain, a trio of young ladies giggled to one another quietly, and another woman in spectacles opposite them checked over some papers.

'I can't believe it's Monday already. Where did the weekend go?' Rachel asked Gemma, who was making herself comfortable on the plastic seat.

'Beats me, Raych. Rough night?'

'Very. Sank two whole bottles of vino. Didn't get to sleep till past three.'

Gemma looked at Rachel's top and noticed a smattering of spew marks over it.

Just then, the members of SMT walked in - single file - and lined up with their backs against the wall.

A lanky, bespectacled gentleman was the stand-out among them. This was David Bland, Deputy Assistant Head Teacher and Head of P.I.P.E (Professional, Institutional & Personal Education). For the sake of clarity, he was in charge of teacher training at Maxwell Gooder's.

Behind him stood Belinda Balfour, the Deputy Head Teacher. She looked like she was in charge - far more physically threatening than Mr Craig Martelle, the actual Head Teacher, who hastily joined the other two.

David offered his hand in the air to catch everyone's attention. At that point, a slow 'I am Spartacus' moment happened - hands of the teachers rose one by one and everyone knew what that meant.

David smiled and turned to the head teacher, Mr Martelle, for his opening remarks.

'Good morning everyone. Just a reminder that tonight is year eight parents evening,' Mr Martelle said. 'As usual, we start at 5:30pm in the main theatre, and will finish at the usual time. So, please do have your class profiles and progress reports printed, so you can answer any questions that the parents may have.'

The entire room muttered quietly, seemingly immediately depressed at the notion of having to deal with parents evening after a long day at work.

'Also just to let you know, teachers of Terry Mills. He's recently been moved - again - to a new foster home. So please try to be gentle with him, as he seems to be finding it difficult to adjust. Thank you. Belinda, I believe you have a message?'

'Yes, thank you Craig.' said Belinda. She stepped forward in such a way that suggested she could well be Maxwell Gooder's head teacher come next summer.

'I just received a phone call from Gareth to tell me that the E-JIT is down until at least midday. He sends his apologies. So please have your contingency classes at the ready if you're relying on the computers or need to print materials. Thanks, everyone. David?'

Rachel rolled her eyes and sighed, clutching the back of her neck.

'Yes. Good morning everyone,' David opened, 'I hope you had a good weekend. Just a couple of brief messages from me today. First, I know it's a bit of a sensitive subject, so we'd appreciate some discretion on this one. When you log into your Electronic Juvenile Information Terminal you'll see that we've put out a warning on the main page to students, teachers and parents that a Gold Ford Fiesta was lurking around the school grounds this morning before the children arrived. It was seen by members of the community approaching a couple of year seven children just outside Ladbrokes at a quarter to eight this morning. We're asking everyone to be extra vigilant. The police have been informed, so there's no cause for concern at this time.'

'That's the third time this month!' came a voice from across the room. 'Who are these people?'

No, Joy, I thought to myself. Just keep quiet. It's just a misunderstanding. It'll be fine. I mean, what are you going to do? Put your hand up and admit that it's your car? No, I don't think so.

David continued. 'So, please, ask your tutor to try and leave in pairs after school and to head straight home. If you could advise any parents who may have any information to please consult their E-JIT from home when it's back online and let us know.'

'Second,' David said, 'as I'm sure you know, Duncan Turner in year eight has his younger sister joining us today in year seven, so I'm sure we'll all make her feel welcome.'

Everyone nodded, in that programmed-to-agree type of way.

'One issue, however, is that her name is Paige, and so—'

Chuckles from most of the teachers bounced through the room. 'Yes, I know, I know. Quite what the parents were thinking, Heaven knows. So please be aware of other, less-kind souls pointing out the same thing.'

I looked over to Rachel, puzzled as to why she was huffing her way through his announcement. Perhaps she was just tired?

'Finally but by no means leastly,' David half-smirked at his own jovial phraseology, 'just a quick reminder that today at 3:30pm we're starting my Professional and Experiential Development Objective - in room 747, which should be finishing at around 4:30. This is mandatory for all, and if you booked the first of three available sessions with E-JIT then you need to be there, as it counts toward your CPD quota for the year. Thank you.'

David stepped back, rather happy with himself.

'Thank you, David.' Mr Martelle cleared his throat. 'I'd like to add also that we've had damage done to the student toilets yet again last Friday. Someone smashed the mirror in the maths department toilets and scrawled graffiti of an explicit nature on the wall. So, please, if you could—'

'What did it say?'

'Mr. Martelle is a cock. But they spelt it with a "K".'

'But cock has a "k" in it?'

'No, it was the first letter—'

'—okay-okay, very good,' interrupted Mr Martelle, 'the point is that we must all be vigilant, particularly if you're on call. Please remember to fill in the sheets and keep an eye on the area at break time. Okay, any other announcements?' Mr Martelle surveyed the seats.

'Yes,' said a teacher in the middle row, whose back was facing Mr Martelle. She leaned around and put her arm over the chair. 'Jenny Slade was approached by two men dressed as a clown on her way home from school yesterday. They followed her on her way home and she's obviously quite distressed about this.'

'Those stupid clown pranksters again! Can't we do anything about this?' asked a teacher.

'Shall we go out and hunt these dickheads down?' suggested another.

'No, better not to provoke the situation. Nevertheless, it's hard to identify men wearing clown make up,' the teacher added, 'but her father is with CID and needs information before these menaces actually do something. Please, if you have any information can you ping me a quick email so I can cobble something for my meeting with Mr and Mrs Slade later today. Thanks.'

'As David said, please ask your tutees to walk home in pairs, and to not engage with anyone in clown make up' Mr Martelle added.

Jeremy, another teacher, stood up and with his notepad. 'Just a quick note from me. As you know, Comms shares its IT suites with RM. Can I please insist that you email estates and ask them to lock the doors if you've been covering, or have moved your class to RM. We had an incident on Friday involving Noel Priestley's left testicle and I'd rather it weren't repeated. Thank you.'

Mutters of approval flew around the room.

'Splendid! Well if that's everything, please have a good week. Do try not to swelter too much in this weather!' said Mr Martelle, as everyone started to shift away from their seats.

'Rachel,' asked Gemma, 'what's David's Productive Education… thing? Do we have to go to that after school?'

Rachel sighed and pulled the wrinkles from her trousers as she walked. 'Another one of David's blue-cloud, blow-bang sessions. We booked the first session with the E-JIT's booking system weeks ago, you remember? Let's just get whatever the hell it is out of the way.'

We all walked to the door. As we did, I was startled by a loud BUZZING noise from above. I nearly dropped my notes.

Rachel giggled. 'That's the school bell. Time for tutor'.

It was tutorial in five minutes' time but weren't in Rachel's classroom. Instead, we were in the neck of a nearby forest about one hundred feet from the playground. Rachel lit a cigarette. She sucked on the end of it like a woman possessed and inhaled deeply, pocketed her lighter and blew out an inordinate amount of smoke from her lungs. She smiled to herself.

'Ahhh. SmokeGasm.' She giggled, as the wafts of nicotine dusted from her mouth. 'Thank the Lord my tutor have gone on study leave.'

'Your tutor? I didn't know teachers have tutors?'

'No, a tutor is a group of students you look after. It's a bit confusing, I know. Teachers don't have their own tutors. They have mentors.'

'Oh okay. And you don't have a tutor?'

'Not anymore. Thank God. An absolute waste of twenty minutes. The last thing you need before an observation. Gives me time to chug a few cigarettes, now.'

It seemed like now was a solemn moment in Rachel's hectic existence. The mood didn't feel particularly conducive to an interview. I struggled for something to say.

'So. You're a teacher?'

'That's right. You're very incisive, aren't you?'

'Thanks,' I said, quickly realising that I had taken her retort at face value. At least it broke the conversational ice. 'How long have you been teaching?'

'This is my second year. I'm an NQT plus one.'

'Right. What is that?'

'It's an acronym.'

'What does it stand for ?'

'A few things. Bull shit is one.' Rachel mumbled, her cigarette dangling from her lips. 'The coconut shy who's thrown all the mundane tasks.' Rachel took a drag from her cigarette and thought aloud.

'Hold on, no. NQT isn't an acronym, is it? It's just initials. Oh whatever, who cares.' Rachel blew out her smoke, defiantly. 'It stands for Newly Qualified Teacher.'

'And the "plus one"?'

'That'd be you!' Rachel smirked. 'Heh. Nah, just kidding. It means I qualified the year before last. This is my second year.'

'How was your first year?'

'Honestly?' she asked, as I smiled. 'A fucking nightmare. Paperwork. Marking. Dealing with numpty parents. Ugh, a fucking nightmare.' Rachel stubbed out her cigarette under her shoe as she delved into her pocket to retrieve another.

'Rachel, if you don't mind my asking, how old are you?'

'How old do you think I am?'

That was a good question. How old was she? She had the wistful grace of a senior teacher, but the youthful pale-skinned complexion of a late twenty-something.

I plumped for the middle ground. 'I don't know. Maybe thirty-eight?'

I was wrong of course, judging by her response - it looked as if I'd wished cancer on her immediate family. Her disappointed gaze soon turned into an evil grin. 'Ah, sod it. I'm thirty-two.'

'Would it be fair to say you've entered the profession later than others?'

'Not really. A lot of people do. I used to work in retail and got to the point where I thought, "if I don't do it now, I never will." so I did,' she revealed.

'You mentioned something about being observed today?'

'Yeah. I have an observation first period.'

'So you are prepared, then?'

'Well, mentally, sure. I'm a sort of fly-by-my-pants-seat

kinda girl. There's not enough time to really prepare. I think the kids appreciate a bit of spontaneity, which is just as well because today is a heavy day.'

Rachel took out her phone and pressed the screen with her thumb. An image of a grid popped up on the screen showing what I assumed was the plan for the day ahead.

'See, this is my timetable. Each period is an hour and twenty minutes, and there are four periods in a day.' I took her phone and expanded the picture on the screen with my fingers. The square marked "P1" has "OBS" scribbled over it.

'It stands for observation,' she explained, 'it's one of three we have during the year, and our appraisal and salary scale depends on them being successful.'

'So you're being officially observed as a teacher in ten minutes' time?

'Yes.'

'How do you know how well you did?'

'There are four grades. Grade one, two, three and four. Four is the worst, and three isn't much better. If you get one of those you'll be assigned a mentor and have to be re-observed.'

'So, grade one is the best?'

'Yes, it means "outstanding" and grade two is "good".

'And you're confident you're on track for that? What grades have you had so far?'

'All grade ones, so far,' she said, matter-of-factly. 'The secret is that it's all really down to two things; the kids liking you, and that they're making progress.'

'Is it really that simple?'

Rachel was veering more on the cocky, arrogant side than the affirmative and assertive teacher I was led to believe I'd be spending the day with.

'I'm making it sound easy, but I suppose you'll see for yourself in a moment!' Rachel said, as she took yet another drag from her cigarette. 'And of course you'll discover it firsthand during period three, won't you?'

'Yes,' I said - my nerves starting to announce themselves in my stomach.

As part of the In Their Shoes series, I have submitted myself to partaking in that profession for a period of time to learn what the job at hand is truly like. I'd always fancied being a teacher, but a lack of a degree has hindered this desire. It's certainly one thing to aspire to a dream when you've had little-to-no actual experience of it, but quite another when you know it's on the cards. Judging by the way she talked about her first class, it seemed as if the quaint movies I'd seen of eccentric, suburban children behaving themselves while the teacher dominated their learning was a thing of the past, if not outright fiction.

'The year nines are a bunch of feral animals, by the way.'

'Feral?'

'Yeah. Well, okay, there are one or two star players like Archie Litchwell or Pauline Norris, but the remainder are—' Rachel stopped momentarily to scramble her thoughts and articulate how she truly felt.

'Well, it's like herding cats, really. Once you've silenced one section of imbeciles, the others play up. And once you've coaxed those nitwits into shutting up, another set of wankers start piping up. It's like spinning plates.'

'Spinning plates? Do they learn anything?'

'Learn? Ha!' Rachel nearly choked on her cigarette butt-end as she laughed.

Surely she's joking, I thought. Surely teachers do not possess such nihilistic thoughts about their students?

'Rarely is the school experience about learning, Joyce—'

'—Joy.'

'Joy, sorry. It's what I affectionately call advanced babysitting. The appearance of learning. With an extra special emphasis on the word appearance, for observation purposes. It's all nonsense. Someday I plan to write a book about it.' Rachel said, with a satisfied reverence. Rachel wasn't joking. There was no punchline. If there was I couldn't feel it and nor did I feel one coming.

Of all the events that were to transpire throughout the day I think it was this alone time with Rachel that sucker-punched me the hardest (although as you'll see this was just the tip of the iceberg).

There was a momentary awkward pause as she inhaled a chunk of her cigarette and looked down at her feet, kicking her shoes slightly off her heel. Rachel, I feel, isn't much for conversation.

'I never really wanted to be a teacher, you know.' Rachel snapped.

'Really?'

'Nup.'

'Then why become one?

No reply. Instead, she tilted her left foot sideways and inspected the sole of her shoe and avoided the question.

As the awkward pause threatened to weave between us, the school buzzer chimed from afar. Rachel looked at her wristwatch and reacted in haste. 'Right, I've got five minutes.'

Rachel flicked her still-lit cigarette into the bush and headed off toward the school yard.

Back in her classroom, Rachel frantically sifted through a textbook. I couldn't quite see the title or the cover but the contents seem to resemble a curriculum.

'3.5 The Elements of Story: 'Irony',' she muttered to herself.

'What is that you're doing?'

'Curriculum. We've basically no manoeuvrability in what we teach, and we have to teach to this book. This module covers irony,' she said as she scanned the text. 'Yeah, pretty basic stuff, I think.'

'And you've not planned this particular class at all?' I asked, somewhat surprised.

'No. Well—' she scrambled for an answer, '—no. I mean, I've taught this a dozen times before, but, no, I haven't planned this actual one.'

'How'd it go last time?'

'Shit. I can't remember—'

'So, how do you know if you've got it right this time?'

'Look, just shut up for a second, will you.'

Obediently, I did as the teacher asked; I shutted up. Rachel slammed the book shut and sprang to her feet, swiping the black white board marker into her hand as she stood in front of it; a move she's clearly rehearsed hundreds of times before.

'Right. We're making this up as we go along.' Rachel insisted. 'What's the definition of irony?'

'Er, I don't know?'

'Come on, think of something!' she barked.

'Uh… when you say or do something that is the opposite of what you meant?'

'Slower, once more.'

Rachel tried to write down what I said on the board, as I slowly repeated myself.

'When you say… or do… something… that is the opposite of what you meant'

Rachel managed to capture the sentence perfectly. 'Gimme an example, quick!'

'Like in that song,' I reached for an answer, hurriedly. 'When it's raining on your wedding, that sort of thing.'

'Okay, okay,' Rachel peered up and glanced over my shoulder. She froze. 'Ah, Clive! Hello!' Rachel's entire demeanour flipped on a dime - from frantic and harassed to romantically professional, as she barged past me and toward this 'Clive' character. He'd clearly seen most of our hastily arranged verbal exchange.

'I hope all is well, Rachel,' Clive said to her, smiling. 'Where would you like me to sit?'

'Oh, anywhere. Anywhere at all!'

'Have you got something for me?' Clive asked.

'Oh yes!' said Rachel, as she swiped an A4 plastic wallet from the table and handed it gently to Clive.

'Oh Clive. Mr Turnbull. This is Joy. Joy-Clive-Clive-Joy.' She said.

Clive shook me by the hand and smiled. In another person's head this may have looked like love at first sight - but nothing could be further from the truth. Well, for me anyway. Clive was a bespectacled man with a receding hair line whose membership to the student union must have expired at least forty years ago.

'Hello Joyce. Nice to meet you.' He said.

'Hello. It's Joy, actually.'

'It certainly is for me,' he retorted with a smile. I was beginning to get a sense of the sort of humour most teachers had (i.e. very little.)

'Clive - Mr. Turnbull - is observing me today. Clive, please do have a seat.'

Rachel beckoned Clive and me over to the corner of her extremely narrow classroom. As I followed him I was curious about the contents of Rachel's bag as I walked past it. Inside were a couple of books on self-publishing and another on writing. I feel somewhat guilty about having looked, but the books were too big for her bag and were screaming out to be noticed.

Eventually, I reached Clive and took a seat next to him. The view of the classroom was about as good as it'll ever be, given the nature of the rectangular - some may say 'lean' nature of the arrangement - but it was what we were working with.

'It's an unusually wide classroom. I don't envy Rachel having to teach here,' remarked Clive, as he perused the open A4 plastic wallets. One document contained a grid of students and their faces, and a bunch of initials that were alien to me. Things like 'STMNT' and 'PP' and so on. Clive began ticking off a prepared checklist on a sheet he had provided.

'What are all these documents?' I asked. Clearly they were related to what we were about to see. Rachel was busy clicking around on her computer, seemingly trying to hurry the machine.

'Oh, these are the observation files. They contain documents about the class. This sheet, for example, gives me an overview of the class's progress and whether or not they need additional support,' Clive said.

'Are these documents really necessary?' I enquired, hoping for a layman's response. 'Isn't teaching all about the environment and what you see firsthand?'

Before we could continue the conversation the school buzzer sounded off. It was followed seconds later by what felt like a thunderous stampede of footsteps that had grown the ability to shout, laugh and scream from the walls behind us. It also cued Rachel to rub her face and click a button on her computer.

'That's true. The documents help build a picture. But it's fairly obvious, for example, if children dislike - or love - the teacher. It's not something you can fake once for an observation. I've observed Rachel a number of times and, happily, she gets on very well with the children.'

Rachel stood up straight and twiddled the pen between her fingers as she eyeballed Clive. Just at that moment, a song started playing over the speakers. On her small monitor I saw a video from YouTube playing. I recognised the song blaring from the speaker system immediately - Ironic by Alanis Morissette.

The kids were outside. The class was about to start.

3
Sar-chasm.
The Lowest Form of Ironie.

The wall clock snapped to exactly 9:00am. I hadn't noticed before, but above the wall clock were the words "Time" and "Passes" in big, colourful lettering. What made it striking were two more words underneath it - "Will" and "You?". A clever little device, I thought.

Alanis Morissette's *Ironic* seemed like a fitting song to usher in the students. Was it usual for teachers to play music in classes, I wondered? Perhaps my understanding of teachers is vastly outdated, but something doesn't sit right. I turned to observe Clive who was busily writing more notes on the documents. I'm not sure that he noticed nor cared that I could see his toe tapping underneath the desk to the beat of the music.

As if on cue, Rachel yanked the door open just as the first verse kicked in. She's clearly done this before. The door revealed a young girl's face staring right at me, peering in from the door frame. A couple of other heads bopped up and down as Rachel leaned against the opened door and surveyed her army of children.

'Okay, quieten down and line up! Against the wall! Now!'

'Miss, are we going on the computers today?' asked the

girl in front.

'Eventually, Phoebe. Maybe.'

'Ah-yeah!' Phoebe exclaimed at the top of her not-inconsiderably loud lungs.

'Shhh! Everyone line up!'

Phoebe bopped her head to the beat of the music, eager to begin the class. Rachel stood back and ushered them all in, single file.

'Okay, in you go. Tables and chairs, NOT computers.'

Twenty-two students filtered into the classroom. When you're actually sitting in it, it can feel slightly intimidating. These year nine students may be thirteen going on fourteen, but some of these boys are fully grown men! Some of the girls have the appearance and physique way beyond their years. The real kicker, though? The randomness of their dispersal into the room. No real order or rhyme to speak of.

They flooded the classroom like a virus smothers its host - but at least it appears they knew which seat belongs to them. It was mildly controlled chaos, as they bopped their head to the puncturing chorus of *Ironic*. I suddenly realised that Alanis has it all wrong; rain on one's wedding day is not actually an irony; rather, a mild misfortune. I was sure I remembered a stand-up comedian making a routine out of exactly this years ago.

The class sat down but were far from settled. One lad sitting at the back, who was quite big and wide-eyed, repeatedly thumped a smaller boy next to him as if he was trying to dislodge his arm from its shoulder socket. It was quite vicious.

'Mason, stop hitting Logan!' barked Rachel from across the room.

A pair of girls busily slapped one another's hands, giggling hysterically. One of them had ink drawings all over her wrist. It seemed that one of them was a butterfly.

'Gaby, Lexie. Stop it!' said Rachel. 'Actually, no, you

two are not to sit next to each other today. Gaby, please move next to Walter.'

Gaby shook her head 'No, Miss.'

'Are you saying "no" to me?'

'Yes I am.'

'Right, you can go outside, then.'

The two girls giggled at each other – it was evident that these two weren't ever going to play ball. Rachel's attention was then drawn to another male duo, sitting next to each other and making a noise.

'Walter, Tyler. Calm down.'

Rachel turned to Gaby and Lexie and eyed them sternly as the music came to a close.

'Okay, you can sit next to each other as long as there's no nonsense. Yes?'

They both nodded their head but smirked with an underlying sense of mischief – there was way more nonsense to come from them.

As determined as Rachel looks, it seemed that this doomed arrangement is the best bet as Clive watched her. It was utterly fascinating from a psychological viewpoint, if nothing else.

Rachel arrived at the front of the class and, as the music stopped, she began. She pointed to the board and banged the pen against it violently; the resultant smash-and-echo once and for all gaining their attention - at least, for the moment.

'Okay. Hands up if you want to answer. What does this word say?'

'Irony!' everyone immediately shouted in unison, and then raised their hands.

Rachel sighed and placed her hands on her hips. It was going to be a long hour.

'I said "hands up" not "everyone shout at once." Let's try that again. Put your hand up if you can tell me what this word means.'

All hands went down.

Clive scribbled some notes on his sheet, and turned to the student sitting nearest to him and whispered in his ear. The student whispered back.

'I thought so. See guys, that's the thing. We think we know what a word means,' Rachel said as she paced slowly around the front of the classroom, making her point. 'But we never really know how to explain it. And that can be a problem in exams. Can anyone give me an example of irony?'

A hand shot up in the air, eager. 'Oooh, Miss!'

'Yes, Phoebe?'

'It's like iron off of the periodic table. It's 'FE'.'

Rachel screwed her face at Phoebe. 'Eh?'

'Dickhead, this isn't science!' barked a male voice from across the room.

'Don't call me a dickhead, you fucking Ostrich!' Phoebe retorted.

'Walter! Next time you swear, you're out. Just calm down.'

'She called me an ostrich, Miss!'

Phoebe was right - Walter did look like an ostrich, with his buzz-cropped hair and gaunt, pale face. Rachel turned to Phoebe. 'Sorry, no, it's not the right answer but it's an insipid guess.'

'Insipid?' enquired Phoebe

'Inspired. I meant inspired.'

'What does "inspired" mean, Miss?' asked another girl.

'It means motivated to do something, Isla,' quipped Rachel. 'Okay, okay, let's start again. Has anyone here ever had their parents say to not do something, even though they go and do it themselves?'

A few hands went up in the air. Phoebe was about to say something when Rachel suddenly shot her down. 'No, Phoebe, remember, hand in the air if you want to speak. Yes, Gary?'

'Yes Miss, like, when my Dad says don't ever smoke, and he goes into the garden to have a cigarette,' he said.

'Okay, that's a good example, Gary.'

'You smoke, don't you, Miss?' snapped Phoebe, smiling.

'No, I don't!'

Rachel was clearly lying to her students. Was she being calculated and clever? Or did she genuinely have the general wellbeing of her students at heart and was trying to set a good example?

An Indian boy leaned in toward Rachel and sniffed loudly.

'You definitely smoke,' he exclaimed.

'Be quiet.'

Isla suddenly had an epiphany. 'So is that what irony is, Miss?' she said, her brain working overtime. 'When you say don't do something but do it anyway?'

'No, not really. That's being contradictory.'

'What's *dicktacontrary* mean, Miss?'

The other children laughed hysterically and began shouting at each other. Har-har, the word "dick" was said.

Rachel ran her hands through her hair and took a deep breath. This literal two second action was enough opportunity for the misbehaviour to penetrate its way in and disrupt the flow. Rachel, like a saint, kept her calm.

'Okay, settle down. Five, four, three, two, one…'

And relax. She had their attention once again.

'Okay, here's an example of irony. Ready?'

The class sat up and paid attention. Rachel stumbled and muttered, her eyeballs searched surreptitiously around the classroom for answers. In reality this part took three or four seconds, but it felt much longer.

'An animal lover who accidentally ran over a dog on his way to an animal charity event. See? Easy.'

Not so for those blinking and confused sets of eyeballs - all twenty of them - that blinked back at her without the faintest idea of what she'd just said.

'No?'

'Ah yes, Miss,' smiled Archie, clocking on to the

meaning 'I get you.'

'Oh thank God. Thankfully someone's brain is working!' said Rachel, as she enjoyed a moment of relief.

'Miss, are you saying I'm a retard?' asked Isla. 'Because my brain is working.'

Rachel ignored Isla at this point to focus on the victory she was about to have with Archie.

'So, for example,' Archie began, 'if, like, someone who worked at Ann Summers was strangled by a rapist with a G-String, that would be irony?'

A deft pause befell what felt like the entire planet. I imagined the postal workers in Manchester dropping tools and staring at Archie wide-eyed; the mime artists in Paris aghast, and the Geishas in Japan stopped fanning themselves and stared at Archie in disbelief.

Back in the room, Rachel was genuinely lost for words.

'Uh, sure. Yes. Not the example I'd have picked, Archie, but yes.'

'Awesome,' said Archie, satisfied with himself.

Phoebe widened her eyes at Archie. I caught her mouthing "fuck you" at him. Rachel didn't notice, but I think Clive did. Archie blew a sarcastic kiss back at Phoebe. Again, this went unnoticed by Rachel, who was too preoccupied with scanning the room for any sign of educational life.

'Anyone else have any other examples? Can we think-'

Rachel stopped in her tracks as she noticed a chubby, ginger-haired student looking forlornly at the table. Upon closer inspection, he was listening to music with his earphones.

'Colin!' Rachel barked, angrily, 'earphones out!'

He exasperated and removed the left earphone, 'you what?'

'Put your earphones away. Have you heard a damn thing I've said all class?'

'No. Tch.' Colin put the earphone back in his ear.

Rachel, surprisingly, let Colin get away with it. It

seemed he wasn't worth her time. I peered over Clive's notes and saw that he had written a few lines on what he'd seen so far. The template on the paper was a box of two halves; the top had 'WWW' written on it, and in the bottom box 'EBS'. The EBS box had more scribbles in it than the other one.

I'm not sure what this meant but any simpleton could deduce that it meant "the good" and "the bad". It wasn't until I locked eyes on Colin who until now had obsequiously and deliberately hidden himself away from the class in plain sight did I realise who "the ugly" actually was.

'Miss,' said Mason, 'so, like, when you're a teacher and you smoke and you tell others not to smoke, then that's irony, isn't it?'

'I can see you've been paying attention, Mason, well done,' said Rachel, utterly sarcastically. 'Thanks,' Mason said, happy with himself.

'No, that's not iron—' Rachel backtracked.

'Ohhh, right,' said Phoebe 'I get it. So irony is, like, when a fisherman who caught a fish throws it back in the sea.'

'Is it actually?' Isla snapped at Phoebe.

'Yeah, 'cuz when—'

'No, no—' tried Rachel, as she fanned her hands out.

'Oh yeah! I get it now!' Isla said, with a smile. 'So it's like when my dad tells me to mow the grass, and I can't be bothered and do a once-over, and it's rubbish, and he says 'well done, great job. Now do it again!"

Isla and Phoebe laughed high fived the fact that they'd mastered the concept of irony which they most certainly had not.

'No, no. Wait,' said Rachel, 'that's not irony. That's sarcasm'

'Is it actually?' asked Isla.

'Like when my grandma caught my brother with his girlfriend and said 'make sure you play safe' and they didn't, and now she's pregnant,' said another voice.

'Did that really happen, Jean-Paul?' asked Isla.

'Yes and my Grandma said to my brother 'I didn't think you had it in you' and he definitely did.'

The entire class laughed. A few of them slapped the table. "Woo! Woo!" - the air of testosterone obliterated the atmosphere as Jean-Paul turned around to collect his accolade.

'But that isn't irony. Those are all sarcastic examples!'

'I'm not a sarcastic example!' Jean-Paul complained.

'You can't say that to us, Miss! We're not sarcastic examples. I should report you!' Isla fluttered her eyelashes, convinced that she'd won the argument.

'Oh for fuck's sake' Rachel muttered under her breath. I suspected that the exasperation wasn't totally meant to be kept under wraps, as Archie saw it and giggled to himself. Rachel and Archie briefly exchanged glances at each other, knowing they were on the same wavelength. The gap in Rachel's delivery opened up a veritable minefield of chaotic opportunism for the remainder of the class.

Angry, Rachel splayed open the doors to her cupboard and slammed a pile of A4 lined paper on the desk as the children filled the room with chaotic noise. She shoved the papers to Isla and gently smiled. 'Isla, can you hand out the papers to the class?'

'No. I'm not happy with you.'

'Are you actualliieee?' Rachel mocked in her best impression of a jumped-up little brat.

'Not talking to you, Miss,' Isla snapped, her self-satisfied response emanating disdain for Rachel as she pretended to write in her book.

Rachel sighed and looked at Phoebe, who in turn shook her head. 'Fine. Fuck it, whatever,' Rachel muttered quietly to herself. Scanning the next row, she landed on a tiny little Oriental girl who smiled back.

'I'll do it, Miss,' the girl said, eager to help. She took the pile and distributed the lined paper one by one as Rachel slowly - despondently - returned to the front of the room and perched her knuckles on the desk.

'Okay, Lizzy is handing out—' Rachel started. It was clearly falling on deaf ears. The commotion was getting unbearable. I was now starting to get very nervous about period three. It was clear that Rachel had lost her grip on the class. My internal alarm bells screamed. Would this happen to me as well?

Rachel's face screwed up. She thumped the desk and screamed. 'LISTEN!' she barked as she stood up straight, meaning business. 'All of you write down one ironic sentence on that piece of paper, and anyone that doesn't will be back at lunch time for a detention to finish it then. Do you understand?'

Everyone shot Rachel a look - she was pissed. Then, quite unexpectedly, a chorus of 'Ooooohs!' filled the room. The students here must possess some aptitude for stealth, as it was virtually impossible to tell who was actually contributing to the sound. Rachel thumped the table once again, which triggered snorting and chuckling from the class; she was nearing the end of her tether.

'I mean it. One sentence. One ironic sentence,' exclaimed Rachel as she started to lose her rag, 'and if you can't do that, then ask me for help,' she finished, sarcastically.

'But Miss, you haven't taught us it,' Isla said, as the class piped up once again, laughing.

'Well, I did try—'

'—well, you should try better, Miss,' Isla retorted, smugly, as she doodled on her notepad.

Clive stood up and hastily gathered his papers. He made for the door and smiled at me as he moved away from our table.

'See you later,' Clive mouthed to Rachel as he silently closed the door behind him.'

Ms Weirdo never does teach us anything!' shouted a random voice.

'Ms Weird is weird!' said another.

Rachel moved to her computer, she sat down and buried her head in her hands. She probably thought she was coming across as pensive. For the first time this morning, I think I felt what being a teacher was really like. Why didn't she hand out detentions? Couldn't she get help? She's lost control of the class for Heaven's sake!

'Weir-do, Weir-do, Weir-do!' chanted the voices in unison, as the tumultuous rustle of scrunched up paper, chatter and chair-kicking echoed through the room.

I felt like crying. I stood up and wandered around the room. I suppose, to them, I was the second observer they clearly hadn't noticed nor given much respect to. I stopped by Phoebe's paper and noticed that Isla had clearly copied from her.

'Hi, Miss. Who are you?'

'Oh, just pretend I'm not here. I'm just observing Rachel.'

'Rachel?' said Phoebe, lighting up.

I realised my mistake. Shit. Shit!

'Hey, EVERYONE! Ms Weir's name is RACHEL! A-haaaa!'

Everyone laughed mightily. And, of course, the chanting of 'Rachel! Rachel! Rachel the Weir-do!' soon followed. Rachel shot me a look of death.

'I think it's better you refer to her as Ms Weir, as usual.'

'Did I get it right, Miss?' Phoebe asked, showing me her paper.

I looked at her work. She'd written this sentence:

Ironie is like when a teacher says you're work is really good but they really mean it is rubbish.

I thought about my response, carefully. 'I think that's more sarcasm,' I said, with a semi-encouraging flourish.

'Ah, shit. So it's wrong?'

'Well, if it were an example of sarcasm it'd be terrific.'

'Are you being sarcastic now, Miss?'

'No,' I said, careful not take her words to heart.

I looked up and saw that Rachel had stood back up and was rubbing her face and checking her wrist watch.'

'Fifty more seconds!' she barked to the students, who were clearly struggling to commit pen to paper.

'Don't worry, Miss,' Rachel said to me, in full view of her students, 'their work is really excellent and brilliant, and they're sooo smart. They'll get it eventually.'

It's rare that you're on the receiving end of sarcasm so pure and angry. It can stop you in your tracks.

'Actually, there's some pretty good examples of it right here.'

'Yeah, I'm sure there are. There's two of them converting oxygen into carbon dioxide as we speak,' she snapped, indicating Phoebe and Isla beneath me. They were busily writing on their sheets, trying to block out the commotion.

'Sarcasm, Miss! That was sarcasm!' said Mason, smiling.

'No, Mason, I'm afraid that was just plain fact.'

'Oh,' he said. 'I thought you were being funny.'

'Stop being strange. Get on with your work.'

Rachel cursorily glanced at some nearby student work sheets. She reached Archie and read his answer to herself. She nearly snorted out phlegm through her nose and tried not to laugh.

'Perfect Archie. Well done!' She patted him playfully on the back. 'Do you mind if I read this out in a moment?'

'No, go for it,' Archie beamed.

I peered over Isla's shoulder as she chatted with Phoebe. She'd given up on the task and had written any old answer down out of formality.

'What's this? Isla, isn't it?' I said.

'Yeah. What's your name, Miss?'

'Jo— uh, Miss Attwood.'

'But your ID card says 'Altwild'' Isla noticed.

'Just call me 'Miss'. What have you written?'

I peer down and see she's written the following: 'An example of irony is when a vegetarian man is forced to eat a chicken and if he doesn't do it another chicken will be murdered.' I was genuinely impressed. I guess that sentence actually was ironic.

'Isla. You nailed it. That's great!'

Isla seemed genuinely shocked, especially as the revelation tore her away from her conversation with Phoebe, who also looked up at me in bewilderment.

'Is it actually?'

'Yes, it's perfect. It's also a bit Catch-22.'

'*Clutch 22*?'

'Never mind.'

Phoebe contorted her face. 'And my one was wrong? That's so peak, Miss!' Phoebe folded her arms and faced away in a huff. It was almost too cute to reprimand.

'Peak?' I uttered to myself. What the hell does that mean? Maybe she meant it's "top" like a mountain summit? I don't know.

Isla nudged me in the ribs, evidently needing some resolution for her work.

'So, Miss Altwild - my sentence is the definition of sarcasm, right?'

'No, not at all. It's perfect. Nothing at all to do with sarcasm.'

'Even though Miss Weirdo said I was a sarcastic,' Isla explained, trying to work out the mechanics in her limited mind. 'I wrote down a perfect sentence for sarcastic, even though she didn't want me to?'

'No, Isla, that would be ironic.'

Isla shot me a glance I'll take with me to the grave. Words I'd use in a sentence to describe her face at this precise moment may include *off*, *knife*, *stab* and *piss*.

Saved by this moment of pure clarity (on my part) and

36

pure incredulity (on Isla's) I think both of us were relieved when Rachel clapped her hands and finally gathered everyone's attention.

Rachel took out her pen and twiddled it between her fingers. 'Now. Who's answering first?'

Everyone's face perked up, hoping they wouldn't be selected. They'd met the pen before.

Rachel spun the pen and it landed on the table. It pointed unapologetically at Lexie. 'Lexie. Your sentence for irony, please,' said Rachel.

'Don't know, Miss,' Lexie pleaded. She'd clearly not done a single second of work.

Rachel thought about her reaction - although I suspect this was an act - and arrived at an answer no-one was expecting.

'Actually, yes - okay, Lexie. "Don't know, Miss" is somewhat ironic, considering you've been in this class and your impervious cranium has resolutely defied any semblance of knowledge to penetrate it. Well done.'

Lexie smiled, happy with this answer - Rachel's tirade careening mightily over her pretty little head.

'Haha! Penetrate!' said Tyler, guffawing like a ferret at his own joke. To be fair to him, it did garner a few titters from the other boys in the class.

But poor Lexie. She had taken Rachel's response to mean that she'd done well. It's rather fitting to note that both Rachel and I looked to Archie to see if that hugely unkind diatribe cloaked in a series of difficult words was lost on *him*, seeing as he was clearly the benchmark of optimum intelligence in this class.

Sometimes a swift closure of the eyelids and accompanying nod of the head conveys everything you need to know. Archie had indeed "got it."

No-one else smiled, though; either out of recognition for the brutal, literate attack, or just plain dough-eyed optimism. Archie was either the smartest kid in the class for his age, or way more mature than the others.

'Archie came up with the best definition so far, I think,' said Rachel, nodding at him to stand up. A voice from out of view murmured the word "boffin" at him.

Archie smiled as he glanced at his sheet.

'Irony is…' he began, 'when a teacher tries to teach a class about irony, but the kids end up learning about sarcasm instead.'

'Perfect. Well done, Archie,' said Rachel. Archie and I exchanged smirks.

It was the first time I saw Rachel exhale since the class started.

The school buzzer went off.

4
One Evil Child & "The Most Boring Person Ever Invented"

'Gaby, open the door!' Rachel demanded. She tried to yank the door handle upward, failing in her literal upward struggle with her side of the door handle against Gaby's full body weight resting down on the handle from the other side. 'Gaby!' said Rachel, starting to get annoyed. 'Open the door, now! Or it's detention!'

Lexie, the girl on our side of the door was giggling just as hard as Gaby.

Eventually, the door handle loosened, and Rachel's hand threw itself upward, nearly knocking her face. Lexie yanked the door open, laughing to herself, and exited the room. 'Bye Miss,' she said, in a way reminiscent of a wounded serial killer setting off on her next quest. The door closed shut.

Rachel smirked to herself, choking back how she genuinely felt. She turned to me and sniggered. 'Well, that was shit.'

The tables were strewn with worksheets that had seen better days. Some were torn up, and it was telling that there were no sheets where some of the more studious students had been sitting; clearly, they'd been taken by the student in question for perusal at a later date.'

So, Rachel, what do you do when you reach the end of a typical period? A chance for reflection?'

Rachel looked at me as if I was burdening her day. 'I have to book time to take a shit. When do you think any teacher has the time to reflect?' She stood up, patting down her trouser pocket.

'I smoke, that's what I do,' said Rachel, as the thundering sound of school kids flew past her room en route to their next class. 'The school will kill me quicker than the fags will.'

Just as Rachel finished the sentence, the large cupboard door slowly crept open and two boys from the class emerged from inside. They had been hiding in there when the bell went and were unable to open the door as the class had filtered out. In the commotion of the kids leaving the room for their next class we hadn't spotted them go in.

They ducked their heads and smiled, hoping to not get told off.

'Do I even want to know? Tyler? Mason?' They shook their heads apologetically, "no."

'Did you hear what Miss and I were talking about, just then?' They nodded their heads, 'yes'. Rachel looked at me and bit her lip, and then looked back at them. 'Well, I won't say anything if you don't. Deal?' They had been caught hiding in her cupboard. Who knows what might have happened if Rachel and I had left the room and locked the door with them still inside. She could've made life very difficult for them. They nodded in agreement.

'Good,' she said, largely happy with the arrangement.

'Now fuck off, the pair of you.'

As Rachel and I walked out of the main English block and entered the playground, a bunch of students came running right past us. This was a fairly big school, and Rachel and I had traversed this patch of land once before - about an hour or so ago - which led us to her secret smoking area. We walked past a couple of boys who were sitting on a bench against the wall listening to music from one of their mobile phones.'

Music is a must to put your stamp on your practise,' said Rachel, as we marched past them. 'Hey, do you want to see something really awesome?'

'Sure'.

Rachel reached into her pocket and took out her mobile phone. She flicked her thumb across the screen as the boys' music blared a few feet away from us. 'It's an app I use all the time,' said Rachel, showing me on her phone. She thumbed the start button, and a pulsing, circular icon thumped like a heartbeat as it clearly listened to the song from the boy's phone.

The phone buzzed, and up sprang a result on the screen: Kodak Black – *Institution*. 'Pretty cool, eh?' asked Rachel. 'I mean, the music is God awful, but if this is what the kids are listening to, then I'll steal it and feign familiarity. This app stores all the music I've sneaked, and creates a play list.'

'That's quite impressive. Does playing music they like actually work?'

'Never seems to. You'd have thought the kids would be like "Ohh miss, you like "insert whatever dick-headed band here" like we do". Never happens. They just take it as read, in their closeted little bubble, that I like it too. But, one day they may surprise me and remark on my fabulous choice of music.'

Rachel pocketed her phone and shouted at the boys as they continued to listen to their music. 'Boys,' she barked, startling them. 'Get to class. Now!' The boys stood up reluctantly and moved off, the track still blaring away, providing precisely the perfect mentality they had toward school. 'I love to shout. Not all the time. But at least once a day helps.'

We marched off in the opposite direction to the boys.

'So, Rachel, can I ask—'

'It's redundant to open a question like that Joy, why not just ask? That's what you're here for, right?'

'Oh', I said, slightly taken aback by Rachel's front, 'sure, I'm sorry.'

'Don't be sorry just come on out with it!'

'Okay. So, do you think being "hip" and "on the kids' level" is important for a teacher?'

Rachel pondered the question as we approached the two trees that promised a nicotine-filled respite from her hectic day.

'Well if they're using words like "hip" and "on the level" then I think they have more pressing issues on their hands,' Rachel replied as she reached into her pocket and took out her cigarette packet.

She glanced over her shoulder to ensure she was out of sight as we stepped past the trees. She placed a cigarette on her out-turned bottom lip.

'When I was at school it was "wicked" and "safe" and stuff like that,' she said as she cupped her left hand over her right and tried to spark a flame.

'I keep hearing the word "peak" a lot today?'

'Yeah,' Rachel said, trying to get her lighter to work. 'It means "out of order".'

'And why are kids ending their sentences with the word "actually"?'

'Oh, that's mainly the girls. It's a—'

Just then, Rachel double-took and lowered her hands. 'Shit. It's period two. I'm meant to be on call!' she exclaimed. 'Quick!'

The cigarette would have to wait as we darted off back toward the school.

We burst through the doors to the main office and up toward the reception area. 'There's that stupid Picasso painting again,' I thought to myself, as Rachel approached the reception counter.

'You're meant to be on call, aren't you Ms Weir?' asked the receptionist.

'Yes, I'm sorry. Got held up with students at the end of P1.

Unconvinced of the excuse she'd just heard, the receptionist passed a walkie talkie through the glass hatch. She also posted an A4 clipboard with a sheet on it, and a pen attached by a piece of string, clipped into a holder to Rachel.

'What channel are we on?'

'I think 11. Hold on,' said the receptionist, as she held her own walkie talkie to her nose. A loud BZZZT static emission blared out through the receptionist's handset, as she inspected it. 'Hello, testing. Coming through?'

'Yep, seems to be working,' said Rachel into her talkie, as she clutched the clipboard.

The receptionist peered over toward me and smiled. 'How's your friend getting on today?'

'Yeah, good. I have to go, we have to go.'

Rachel turned around and nodded in the direction of her classroom, and we both began to walk. As we moved, I noticed that Rachel was fiddling with the volume dial, turning it right down. 'Okay, that's the talkie set,' she said, clipping it to the side of her belt. 'Let's go get that coffee now, shall we?'

'Who was that on reception?'

'Dunno.'

No sooner had we reached the top of the stairs, than we were in the IT staff room. There was no-one in the room - just us. The cup Rachel had left on the counter and open coffee sachet leaning against it had gone untouched. Rachel flicked the switch on the kettle and pulled out a mug from the tray.

'You want a coffee, Joy?'

'Sure,' I said. 'So, what exactly is "on call"?'

'Everyone has it at least once a week in place of a

period. Basically you run around like a blue-arsed fly, sorting out unruly students and escort them to the LEO. Or maybe you'll have to usher a visitor to a meeting with teachers. Things like that.'

'What's LEO?'

'Ah. It's the Lowering Expectations Office. It's the modern-day equivalent of the Headmaster's office, if you like. Kids get told off in there, given detentions and put on report. That kinda thing.'

'Right. So, on call sounds like it's chock-full of adventure?'

'Yeah. Yeah, I guess it does sound adventurous. But it's just another pain in the sphincter that ensures work gets done at home, rather than at work.'

'Really? Seems to me to be an ideal time for getting other stuff done if it's not too busy?'

Rachel shot me a look. 'Have you ever tried to sit down and write one of your books with your husband and kids running around distracting you?'

'No,' I quipped, sensing her strange vocalism on the subject, 'but then, I'm not a writer'.

'Oh. Well, anything that requires concentration? Okay, would you, for instance, instigate a sexual romp with your boyfriend if you knew your mum was going to knock at the door in the next hour?'

'Well, no.'

'Well. There you go.'

The kettle clicked to a stop and rumbled, bellowing steam. It was as if it were laughing at Rachel's victory over her analogy. She picked up the kettle and poured the boiling water into her flask, and then poured some into my mug.

'It's the main reason I do all my marking at home. I can't do it here, what with the emails and student interruptions. Of course, you have to factor in the unwritten "procrastination factor", too - the mental dexterity it takes to actually settle down and focus,' she said, passing me my mug of steaming hot coffee.

'I suppose that makes sense.'

Rachel held her mug up to mine. 'Cheers!'

We clinked mugs. She smiled and pursed her lips as the piping hot mug rim threatened to scald her top lip.

BZZZT. 'Hello, on-call?'

The shock of the announcement caused Rachel to tip most of the contents of her mug over her top. 'Shit! Shit! Shit!' She exclaimed, waving away her hand, dripping with coffee.

'Come in, on-call?' said the talkie. 'Are you there?' Rachel held the button on the side. 'Yes, this on call, what is it?' Rachel asked, patting down her front with a dirty tea-towel from the table top.

'What was that about shitting, on-call?' asked the talkie. 'Nothing, sorry,' said Rachel, visibly distressed. 'Just an accident.'

'Room 318, maths. Master Mills is playing up again.'

Rachel suddenly became very put-out.

'Shit. Terry Mills' she muttered to herself whilst holding down the talkie button. 'Okay, I'm on my way'.

I followed behind Rachel as we barrelled down what looked like an endless vanishing point of canvas art-laden walls and random student work containing diagrams, numbers and charts. Yet more strange Picasso-esque art adorned the walls, and the unmistakable whiff of TCP hung in the air, although I had no idea where the medical office was - if they even had one?

The room numbers passed by sequentially and evenly; 310, 312, 314 and so on. We eventually arrived at room 318. A little boy was standing outside the door, facing the wall, picking apart a poster with his finger tips. He seemed utterly despondent - he pressed the side of his body and blazer across the wall like a crap makeshift rolling pin. Rachel approached him within a safe distance and folded her arms. She cracked open an unusual posh accent and theatrics.

'Master Mills, as I live and choke. What seems to be the problem?'

'Nuffin'.'

'Terry, what are you doing out here?' Rachel asked, returning to her normal voice.

From inside the room, a few blinking eyeballs from students looked on at Rachel and Terry, and then at me, to try and see what was happening. Clearly this wasn't the first time that this has happened, and their eyes averting back to the white board suggested it may not be the last, either.

'Excuse me, students,' said a voice from within the classroom.

A petite, pale-skinned teacher emerged from the classroom with a white board marker in her hand. She looks angry but unsurprised. 'Terry, are you going to do the activity?'

'No,' said Terry. 'It's boring.'

'Is Terry still not getting it right, Mrs Jackson?'

'No, Ms Weir. He's not. Well, it'll just have to be a trip to the Biscuit Tin, won't it Terry?' quipped Mrs Jackson. Terry continued to pick away the paint on the wall.

'Won't it, Terry?' repeated Mrs Jackson, who looked at me and smiled. She turned to Rachel. 'Sorry Ms Weir, I've a class on. Can you take him to the LEO for me. Let Ms Hendricks sort him out.'

'Certainly Mrs Jackson. Okay. Terry, come with me, please,' ordered Rachel. Terry continued to roll the side of his body across the wall, picking at some work displays.

'No,' Terry mumbled.

'You know what will happen if you end up at the LEO with Ms Hendricks, don't you?' Rachel asked, knowing he knew the answer. 'You'll end up in the biscuit tin all week.'

'The biscuit tin?' I asked, confused. The school was full of bizarre jargon.

'You wanna tell Miss what the biscuit tin is, Terry?'

Rachel said. 'No! It's gay!' was his somewhat predictable, if vulgar, response.

Rachel folded her arms and feigned a sigh. 'Miss, the biscuit tin is where naughty little boys like Terry, here, are sent to. They sit on their bum all day, or sometimes all week, on their own.'

Terry didn't seem to care. He'd probably spent more time in this biscuit tin than he did in classes. Terry continued to absentmindedly pick the displays.

'Terry, don't pick at the artwork,' said Rachel. To no avail, of course. For all intents and purposes, this seemed to be a situation where - if you wanted a kid to do something - you should probably instruct him to do the exact opposite.

I could see I was starting to think along the same lines as Rachel, as the feisty, contrary oppressor inside her finally kicked in.

'Terry,' she said, amused at his continued defiance, 'keep on peeling apart the artwork,' she said, in the hope he'd do the opposite.

Her ploy backfired spectacularly. The evil little tyke yanked on the artwork and tore it off the wall. 'Terry!' shouted Rachel. 'Stop that!'

'Eurgh! Your breath stinks!' Terry yelped into her face, disgusted. She grabbed him by the arm and wrestled with him.

'My breath does not stink!' she shouted. Terry yanked his arm away and screamed.

'Don't touch me! SHE'S TOUCHING ME!'

Terry darted off down the corridor, and backed up against the wall by room 310, about ten feet away from us. There was a mild hint of a Mexican standoff about the situation; two fully grown adults versus one malignant tumour of a child. All that was missing was an Ennio Morricone theme, and the set-up would have been complete.

'You told me to do it,' he barked. 'You stupid bitch!' He

turned around and began picking apart another piece of student wall art. Rachel clenched her teeth, her instincts telling her not to scream back nor cause a scene, for fear of losing A) her rag, and B) her job, in full view of children trying to figure out their times tables.

Suddenly, I witnessed something I wasn't expecting. Rachel snapped into calm mode, and slowly - but very surely - paced toward him, as if she was The Terminator. She hunched her shoulders and, finally, displayed some glimmer of a real, seasoned pro, resisting a genuine 'sod off' from a mouthy little brat. 'Terry,' she insisted, 'step away from the wall. You're coming with me to see Ms. Hendricks.'

Just as she reached out to him, he darted off down the corridor as quick as his little villainous legs could carry him. These little rats can't half run, I remember thinking.

'Yeah, but she'll never do anything, anyway! She never does! Fuck off!' Terry's voice echoed, as he hightailed it up the nearest flight of stairs.

Rachel and I turned to face each other. We then faced forward - clocking Terry's feet disappear up the stairs. We darted after him.

Have you ever seen a movie where two fully grown adults are chasing after a putrid little ghost through the labyrinthine corridors of an 18th century building? It felt like that as we stepped forward, looking for Terry. Rachel and I traversed the corridors of the first floor in the science block. It felt like something out of a sub-par teenage slasher movie that only managed to score a 12% fresh rating on Rottentomatoes.com

'Terry,' yelled Rachel, 'stop being an idiot and come out.'

Rachel peered into room 881S, a science room. Rows of students on stools were quietly completing a test in front of their handsome teacher as he sat at his laptop taking the register. He turned around and smiled at Rachel as we walked in, silently.

'Ah, hello Ms Weir. You okay?'

'Hello Mr Fiddle! I'm looking for Terry Mills, have you seen him?' A few of the students glanced up at us, taking a fleeting break from their exam.

I turned to Rachel and mouthed 'Mr Fiddle?!' at her, thinking this poor sod must regularly be the subject of unwanted distress due to his surname. She shrugged her shoulders and looked back at him.

'No, although someone did run past a minute or so ago, but I didn't see who it was,' said Mr Fiddle, guffawing. 'If I see him I'll let you know. Are you on call?'

Rachel waved her walkie talkie as confirmation. 'Just let me know if you see him.'

Rachel and I walked down the science corridor and kept on scanning for our little deserter. It may seem trite and over-egged, but I could tell that this was one of the few times Rachel felt that her job was worth doing. I mean, to me, this doesn't feel like one of the reasons why someone would ever become a teacher.

During my limited time with Rachel - a couple of hours or so, at this point - I was beginning to sense the showman in her, deep down inside. She didn't conform to the stereotypical teacher typeset you'd expect - rigid, studious and somewhat maternal. Right now, in fact, she looked like a prison guard surveying her territory. All that was missing was a torch and firearm in her side pocket, where the walkie talkie was.

Rachel stopped. It was as if she'd had an epiphany. 'Oh, you know what. Forget it. Let him go,' she said. 'I'll just put it in the report. Life's too short for this bollocks,' she said. She took out the clipboard from under her arm and slapped it on the wall in front of her face. 'Jesus Christ, can you imagine doing this when you're sixty? Running around after little bastards like Terry Mills? Fuck that.'

She chewed the lid off the pen, and began filling in the sheet.

'Incident, Terry Mills. Maths room,' she said to herself. She looked at me and smiled. 'Nature of incident?' she mused.

'Defiance?' I contributed.

'Uh-huh. Being a prick,' she said as she wrote it down, 'but it's not enough. Let's make some shit up.' She began writing more words on the sheet as if she were signing Terry's death warrant.

'Right. Terry pulled apart some artwork from the wall, and when challenged, he called me a 'stupid fucking bitch',' Rachel narrated as she wrote, happy with her response. 'Mills then ran off toward the science corridor and I lost him. Recommend immediate referral to Biscuit Tin, Ms. Hendricks,' she finished writing.

She slid the business end of the pen into her mouth, and into the lid between her teeth. 'Done.'

'But he never said the word "fucking"?'

'No, I know. But it makes it sound more dramatic,' she said. 'Inserting sexual adjectives into the mix makes him seem like an even bigger prick than he actually is. No amount of made-up vulgarity will truly elucidate just how big a prick he actually is,' she said, happy with herself. 'Ugh, I just wanna go home. This is so tedious. C'mon, let's go.'

We walked off toward the school yard when, practically out of the blue, we were greeted by the holiest of holy sights - Terry had been accosted by a member of staff. And not any old member of staff, either.

'Ms Hendricks!' Rachel exclaimed as we approached the pair.

'Hello Ms Weir. I understand Terry was kicked out of maths and defied your instructions, is that not right, Terry?' asked Ms Hendricks.

'Yes, that's not right Miss,' said Terry.

'Don't get smart with me, young man. How'd you like me to call home and tell your mum what's just happened?'

Terry just shrugged his shoulders. 'I don't care. She's

not my real mum, anyway.'

Ms Hendricks smiled at Rachel and me. 'I'll handle this, Ms Weir. Thanks for your help.'

Rachel tore off the top sheet from her report and handed it to Ms Hendricks. 'Here you go.' Ms Hendricks took the paper and marched Terry off toward a flood of sunlight that screeched through the double door windows at the end of the corridor.

For a brief moment it looked like the pair of them had died and were going to heaven. Rachel elbowed me in the ribs, jolting me out of my mire.

'Right, time for a smoke. Hopefully that's the last wanker we have to deal with.'

Back in Rachel's "main office" and - as redundant as this will surely read – Rachel had a cigarette on the go. Loud birdsong surrounded us from all directions. I scanned around the forest and noticed a building with smashed windows.

'What's that?' I asked.

'Oh, that's disused. No-one lives there anymore. I heard the caretaker lived there before he died, and I don't think anyone occupies it anymore. It's empty.'

Rachel just about managed to light her cigarette, nearly dropping the clipboard. 'Till I'm in my sixties? Jesus Christ, no,' Rachel whispered to herself. She closed her eyes and bit her lip. I chuckled, as if to say 'Yeah! Tch! Who'd want that!' She took another drag and held the smoke deep into her lungs.

BZZZT. The sudden jolt of the talkie caused Rachel to cough out and splutter, rather than exhale. She wheezed and choked for air, wafting the smoke away.

'You may not live to see your sixties, at this rate,' I joked.

'Fuck you, Joy,' Rachel joked.

'Hello, on-call?' asked the talkie.

Rachel held down the button, clearing her throat.

'Fuck's sake... yep, this is on call. How can I help?'

Silence. 'On call, can you not use curse words on this channel please?'

'Sorry about that,' said Rachel, clearing her throat.

'On-call. Are you smoking?' asked the talkie.

'Uh. No?'

'You're coughing. Are those birds I can hear tweeting?'

'No, look, what do you want? Can't you see I'm busy?'

'I can't see anything, I—'

'I know, it was a joke,' Rachel sighed, enacting the global sign for masturbation with her right hand at me. 'Thick as a plank, this woman.'

'Main lecture theatre,' the voice on the walkie-talkie said. 'We have a primary school visiting for an external theatre production and one of the students' dads is on his way to pick him up for a doctor's appointment.'

Rachel clicked the talkie. 'What's the kid's name?'

A small pause, as Rachel looks at me, pursing her lips, impatiently.

'It's... "Ache-Arse", but...' offered the talkie.

'Arse ache, more like.'

'No, it's ache arse. But,—'

'—is that all there is? Is that her full name?'

'No. There's ache arse, but—'

'—but? But what?'

'Butt. Ache arse—'

'Will you stop saying ache arse!' Rachel snapped.

'No, honest! That's what it says here.'

'Spell the first name for me.'

'A-K-A-S.'

'That's Ay-kass, you dummy. It's an Indian name. Ay-Kass. Butt?' said Rachel into the talkie, rolling her eyes. 'Honestly, where do we find these idiots?'

'I'm sorry?' said the puzzled voice over the talkie.

'Is Butt the surname?' Rachel bellowed into the talkie, impatiently. A few seconds trundled by.

'Forget it. I'm on my way.'

'Thank you on-call!'

'Yeah fuck you, too,' snapped Rachel as she clipped the talkie to her belt.

Rachel kicked her shoes as she shoved her right hand into her pocket. 'There must be six hundred kids in there. Thank God this one's Indian. We've a better chance of finding her.'

Rachel took out a packet of chewing gum and offered me a stick. I shook my head, as she opened up one for herself and threw it in her mouth. 'Bad breath, by the way? Me? He's the evillest boy in the world, that kid.' We headed off toward the main building.

Rachel and I approach Maxwell Gooder's Main Theatre. This area of the school was brand new to me. Until now I'd only seen the mezzanine, English, IT, maths and science blocks. I'd seen Rachel's "main office" three times. I'd figured out where the most important parts of the school were.

To the west of the school a whole new world presented itself. A second playground, with huge football markings in a segregated section of the corner of the playground. I was suddenly taken aback by just how big Maxwell Gooder's Comprehensive School actually is.

As we walked through the playground a man came running toward us from the other end. It was a tall, lanky figure. I couldn't make out who it was but Rachel certainly could.

'See him over there?' Rachel whispered.

'Sort of.'

'I hate him,' Rachel snapped, voraciously. 'Prepare yourself for the most boring person ever invented.'

As the figure came into focus, I immediately clocked the wire-frame glasses, receding hairline and pompous smirk. He was at the morning meeting, but I couldn't remember his name. 'Quick, keep walking, pretend you haven't seen him—'

'Helloooo Ms Weir!'

Rachel closed her eyes and bit her lip. 'Shitsticks.'

'A quick word if I may, Ms Weir.'

Rachel stopped dead in her tracks, closed her eyes and sighed. She'd been caught in the tractor beam of someone she clearly wanted nothing to do with. She opened her eyes, turned to face him and smiled, somewhat over-exaggeratedly.

'Mr David Bland! Well Helloooo to you, too!' she quipped, feigning affection. 'To what do I owe the honour?' She shot me a look of suicide just as quick as she faced him again, all smiles and champagne receptions.

'Ms. Weir, did you get my email regarding a quick meeting at break time?'

'Uh, no? I didn't get an email,' said Rachel, as she pulled out her smart phone and examined it.' No, no email.'

David sighed, patronisingly - in a way that suggested that she required some sort of professional pity. 'Oh, that's peculiar. I sent it about twenty minutes ago?'

'Right, well, I'm on call, so I wasn't able—'

'--yea-huh sure. It's just that we need an urgent chat. I'm keen to expedite it and rectify the issues at hand before it escalates into something of a Sisyphean struggle.'

We both stared at him in utter bemusement.

'Huh?' Rachel was barely able to hold back her incredulity.

'Yea-huh sure. So, shall we say eleven-forty this ay-emm, start of break time, in your room?' asked David, as he dramatically threw out his arm and checked his wristwatch.

'Fine,' offered Rachel, stepping away. 'Sorry, I'm on call, gotta get to the theatre.'

'Yea-huh sure. No problem. Have a wonderful on call!' David smiled at her. He marched quickly toward the canteen area. I was awe-struck by his slightly effete movement as he walked.

I shrugged that off to find Rachel had so successfully extricated herself from his presence that she was practically at the door of the theatre.

I ran after her.

Rachel yanked the large, hulking door to the theatre wide open. 'Okay, let's find this pain-in-the-arse, or whatever her name is.' The door squealed like an old, rickety wooden brontosaurus as it opened.

'Who here has heard of the term "gender fluidity"?' boomed an over-excited male voice from within the bowels of the theatre.

We stepped forward and disappeared into the darkness.

5
Ruby Loves the U-bend

It's hard to describe the interior of the theatre as was in virtual darkness. A sliver of sunshine poured through the window of the giant double doors leading into the hallway, but the hallway itself was dark. At the far end was another set of double doors. Behind them, we could hear a performance of some description. A voice of a man talking loudly, accompanied by music I didn't recognise.

Rachel and I carefully stepped forward. 'Shhh!' Rachel said to me, with her index finger over her lips. She raised the walkie-talkie in her other hand and dialed the volume right down to zero. 'We can't have this going off in here,' Rachel whispered to me, as the talkie static clipped off into silence.

She opened the left door, allowing the volume of the production to resonate around us. We stepped in.

The theatre was awash in pink and purple lights. A huge elevated stage loomed to the right hand side, as the curved arrangement of plastic seats enclosed the stage itself. There must have been more than five hundred seats, all filled with little, well-behaved human beings. The smaller ones were lined up at the front - and for a high school, they appeared to be *very* small. No older than nine years old.

Rachel and I snaked our way along the sidelines and past faceless standing patrons as the show continued in front of the stage. Yes, in front of the stage; not actually on it.

I had no idea why they weren't using the actual school stage. The arrangement had a backdrop of a crudely drawn house on a large white sheet; the windows had been drawn on in crayon. The door was the same height as the performers. No expense was spared save for the professionally designed banner that advertised this travelling theatre company's wares. Fun-Tastic Fact-Toidz - or FTFT for short - as per the advertising in bright, weak red lettering behind them. They'd even managed to secure FaceBook, Twitter and Instagram logos next to it, as well as their '.biz' extension for the website.

Rachel stepped backward, and ended up standing beside someone she knew; a stern-looking woman, with a very square and hulking body.

'Hi Belinda.'

'Hello, Ms Weir.'

'What are we watching?'

'It's show about gender fluidity for the year sevens and Chrome Hill year sixes.'

'Sounds fun.'

'It'd better be. It cost us five hundred quid.'

I looked at the 'stage' just as a tall, chiseled actor with greased hair jumped out from the door of the house with his arms outstretched.

A song started playing and the man moved to the rhythm of the tune. I recognised the tune immediately. *You Don't Own Me* by Grace.

'Hi everyone,' he said, patronisingly. 'My name is Troy, and these are my friends - Ophelia, and Tarquin. And we are Fun-Tastic Fact-Toidz!'

Ophelia, a svelte actress, appeared beside him and waved at the kids. She was dressed as a man in trousers and a shirt. Tarquin, equally as chiselled as Troy, stood the other side dressed in a skirt and blouse. It looked like he was wearing lipstick but it was hard to tell from this distance.

'We're here to tell you all that it's okay!' said Troy, as he lent his palm to Ophelia. 'Yes, Troy, it's okay. To be different!' Then, Tarquin stepped forward. They both held Troy's hand and squeezed tightly.

'Like me,' said Tarquin, putting on a strange effeminate voice. 'I'm different,' he insisted, looking at the children in the front row. 'And it's okay for you to be, too.'

'But Tarquin is my best friend,' Troy pondered, over-acting, as the lights dimmed down to a spotlight on his musing. 'I always thought he was a boy, but he likes wearing ladies' clothes! He looks like a girl!'

The kids remained silent as the show continued. Were they soaking all this up obediently, or were we witnessing the training of six hundred children for the Jeremy Kyle Show five years from now?

As Tarquin acted all sad some of the children in the audience started to laugh - as children would do.

'It's just not fair,' Tarquin said, as the music faded down. 'All I ever wanted to be was accepted for who I was. Sure, I was born a boy with all the wonderful tools that a boy has!' The spotlight sequestered into a blue pulsing beam. 'I had action men, played video games on my Playstation 4 and I really, *really* like other girls!'

Ophelia emerged in a school uniform, wearing trousers and a dodgy sprayed-on five o'clock shadow. Burrowed deep into her eyes was a clear, jolting regret that screamed "three years at RADA - for this!" But maybe that complaint was just in my mind. The theatre is good at playing tricks on you.

'Hey, Tarquin,' Ophelia shouted.

'Yes, Ophelia?'

'You look like a girl, you must be a faggot! We should rename you to Chiquita, or something!'

Troy interrupted them. 'No Ophelia. "Faggot" is a derogatory term, and we should never use it.'

'How about "bummer"?

'No, Ophelia. That's a bad word, too.'

'"Poo-stabber"?'

The children laughed at the word "poo". Troy waved his hands, alerting that none of this was okay.

'No, Ophelia. All those words are derogatory, and can hurt people who are different.'

Ophelia acted puzzled and pressed her index finger to her lips. 'But why on Earth not, Troy? He is a faggot after all!'

'No,' Troy replied, posing. 'Faggot is a bad word, so we never use it. Instead, we use the word homosexual.'

Ophelia played upset, held her palm to her forehead and posed, dramatically. 'Oh, I'm so confused!'

'I'm not even a homosexual, though, Ophelia,' announced Tarquin. 'I'm just so confused over my gender.'

Ophelia cottoned on and her face lit up. 'In which case, you *must* be a homosexual!'

The lights tipped up, full beam, to allow Troy to shove his way through the middle of them, stopping the scene. 'You see kids, there's a huge difference between sex,' said Troy, as a smattering of children giggled (tee-hee "sex"!) 'And gender! For example, you can be born a boy… or a girl. But your *gender* is how society sees you and how you integrate into it.'

'Put your hand up if you know what 'integrate' means!' Ophelia buoyantly asked the audience.

No hands went up.

I stepped toward Rachel as she looked at me. She closed her eyes and shook her head in disapproval as the performance continued.

'Right,' Rachel mouthed at me, sliding her chewing gum into the inner wall of her mouth. 'Let's find this Akas girl and get out of here.' I nodded, and walked with her to the left side of the auditorium.

As we approached the far end of the theatre, we saw about twelve long, long rows of children watching the performance - each row bookended with a seated adult.

Each adult was suffering this God-awful show with folded arms and occasionally turned their head to 'shush' a child who was making a noise.

In what felt like a sea of frightening Wiltshire Aryan faces lit up by the dimmed house lights, neither Rachel nor I could see one that was not white.

'I can't see her,' whispered Rachel. 'I'll ask this chap.'

Rachel approached the nearest adult and gently tapped his shoulder. 'Excuse me, I'm a teacher at this school. I was wondering, do you have a student called Arse — uh, Aykass, here?'

The adult looked up at her and smiled. 'You mean Akas. Yes, I think so.'

The adult leaned forward and scanned his own row. Rachel had made the right choice in working from the back row, forward; it was far less disruptive. There was simply no point going from the front end backward in case you have to filter through the row of seats and obstructing people's view of the show.

After a bit of scanning, the adult - and Rachel, and I - spotted Akas almost immediately. It was a boy - a chubby little nine year-old not three seats away from us. Sometimes you just can't see the wood for the trees (not that I'm suggesting a brown complexion should be compared with tree bark, you understand.)

Praise the Lord! He's been located. We shifted up behind Akas. Rachel bent over from behind and tapped him on the shoulder. Her attention was drawn to the leaflet in his hand - a Fun-Tastic Fact-Toidz! Leaflet crudely altered in biro to read "Fuck-Tastic Fuck-Tardz!"

Rachel swiped the leaflet out of Akas's hand, which at once startled him and announced the presence of an adult in his life.

'Uh, Miss!' said Akas, turning his head over his shoulder to face her.

'You think this is clever, Akas?' she whispered. His nearby friends all face away, temporarily disassociating themselves from their "clever" friend.

'It was not me' said Akas, in his adorable broken English. 'I found it,' he insisted, turning his head to his lap apologetically.

Chiquitita by ABBA begun playing as the actors launched into a dance; pretending to cry and hug one another.

'Well, whatever, Akas,' Rachel insisted. 'I don't find it very fun-' she said, as she's interrupted by a BEEP-BEEP noise from her phone.

A row of heads turned around to see what the noise was, and immediately pinned the blame on Rachel as the glow of her phone lit up her face.

'Sorry,' she mouthed to the heads as, disgruntled, they returned to watch the show.

The phone showed this email message:

From Mr. D Bland; 10:51am. Subject: Urgent Meeting req. Dear Rachel, need to meet urgently at break. Please confirm.

As Rachel closed her mouth and sighed, her chewing gum dropped out of her mouth and landed dead-square in the middle of Akas's hair turban! Rachel froze solid. Her entire career must have flashed before her eyes. Worse still, no-one other than Rachel and I saw it.

If you're not sure what a hair turban looks like, imagine a hair bun - but this time, coiled into a sort of bird's nest - in this case held by a band. Its purpose is to retain hair on the individual's head, as it cannot be cut off for religious reasons.

In this case, Akas is clearly Sikh. As of five seconds ago, its new purpose is to secure a thoroughly chewed nugget of peppermint gum.

A minute felt like a year.

Rachel's face remained frozen, as did mine. Her eyeballs peeled to the right of their sockets and stared right at me. 'What do I do now!?' her eyeballs shouted. I stared back. What does one do in this situation?

Well, what any great teacher would do.

Nothing.

Outside, Rachel and I escorted Akas - and his hair turban with chewing gum in it - across the school yard, and toward reception. Akas walked a couple of steps in front of us, feeling very ashamed of himself for the leaflet misunderstanding. The problem was that Rachel and I are about five foot six, and Akas - a mere nine years-old - was roughly chest-height to us. Maybe four foot eight, if an inch. This effectively meant that we had a front-row view of the chewing gum nestled - nay, perfectly ensconced - in the very centre of his hair; like the most perfectly mounted bird's egg the world has ever not seen.

As we walked, Rachel couldn't control her face and began snorting with laughter. This, in turn, set me off. Rachel chewed her lip and snorted once again through her nose, which made me choke back and clear my throat.

Akas immediately turned around and put his hands on his hips. 'Are you laughing at me?'

'No-no-no,' implored Rachel. 'no, sweetie, we're not.'

'Good. I shan't be tolerating racism,' added Akas, as he gracefully spun around one hundred and eighty degrees and continued marching forward, his dignity restored.

Rachel and I lost our shit. It took her a good thirty seconds to stop laughing and to regain her composure. I nearly pissed myself. Akas stood waiting, thoroughly annoyed and - it must be said - entirely in the right.

We arrived at reception and were greeted by a much larger version of Akas, wearing a suit.

'Son!' said Akas's father, 'Come now, we're going to be very late.'

'Sorry father, I didn't know the field trip was today.'

'Well, these very kind ladies assisted me in my phone call to find you. Come, son, we must go. Thank you, ladies.'

'You're very welcome Mr. Arse-Khan.'

Akas's father turned to me and smiled 'And who are you, Miss?'

'It's Joy Attwood. Hello,' I said as I offered my hand for him to shake. *'In Their Shoes'.*

His father just stared at me uncomfortably and gripped his son's hand even tighter.

'Let's get out of here, son.' Akas's father was clearly deeply unimpressed by me.

No sooner had he said that, that he noticed the chewing gum on top of his child's head. He scowled at his son, who looked up with a gentle, beady-eyed look of an angel. He had no idea what his father had seen. I felt so guilty. I wanted the ground to open up and just swallow them both.

To pour salt into the ethical, gaping chasm of flesh, Akas spread a smile across his face as he looked at his father. This was enough to convince Mr. Butt that his child genuinely had no idea what was going on; a sort of wide-eyed, childish innocence.

Mr Butt slowly looked up at Rachel and then at me. He narrowed his eyebrows, grabbed his son's hand, and slowly walked away.

Rachel and I breathed a sigh of relief. But said relief was broken immediately by the sound of cackling and screaming from the annexe near the playground.

As Rachel and I hastily jogged toward the annexe that separated the maths department from the playground, I took the opportunity to check my watch. Time had flown by - it was 11:25am, and I felt my stomach growl.

Ever the professional journalist, I kept this information to myself as we head toward source of the commotion. We arrived at the annexe toilets just outside the girl's toilet door. There was a familiar song playing from within, and it was evidently very loud if we were able to hear it from the other side of the door.

Rachel looked at me, and clipped the talkie to her belt. 'These are always a barrel of laughs.'

We walked inside.

I follow closely behind her. I recognised the track that's playing - The Next Episode by Dr Dre and Snoop Dogg.

Inside, we navigated through the small corridor - barely ten feet long - that snaked 45 degrees around and revealed the source of the noise. A faint waft of marijuana drifted toward us.

The cackling and groaning continued. When Rachel peered around the corner, her eyes widened and her jaw dropped.

Two pasty-faced teenage boys, around fourteen years-old, dressed only in their underwear were passing a badly-rolled joint between themselves and were clearly high off their nipple-ends. Their uniforms were strewn across the floor - a couple of pairs of trousers, two shirts, a blouse and skirt, four individual grey socks and a soaking wet pair of white knickers. A mobile phone was perched on the edge of one of the sinks playing the music very loudly.

'Ms Weir!' said one of them, as he sputtered. 'You wanna toke, Miss?' He laughed and coughed at the same time; the smoke clearly interfering with his bloodshot eyes.

'What do you think you're doing, Blake?' Rachel bellowed over the music.

'What does it look like, nigga?' he said as he sucked down on his joint and offered it to her. He kept the smoke held in his lungs.

The other boy piped up as he scrambled off his knees and to his feet. 'Miss, Blake thinks you're hot,' said the boy.

'Fuck off do I,' Blake retorted, bellowing the deeply-held smoke from his lungs and into Rachel's general direction. 'Ah c'mon miss, take a drag. I promise I won't grass you up to Mr Martelle!' he giggled, slightly losing his balance.

Upon closer inspection, I could see that Blake was rather "relaxed" given the circumstances, both in his demeanour and in the underwear department. This was a boy who's familiar with the result of puberty.

It takes a lot to shock me, but I was on the verge of

being so. The same could not be said for Rachel who ordinarily might have screamed for the police at this point. She was, however, momentarily distracted by some daubing on the wall behind Blake. He moved away to playfully 'knock' his friend between the legs as hard as he could.

'Ergh, you fucking nonce! Touchin' my dick, you fuckin' fag!' yelped his friend.

My attention was caught by big, capitalised graffiti on the wall. It read thus:

Mr. Martelle is a Kock
Ms Weir(do) is a Home(o)

Rachel's silence wasn't to be taken as flabbergast at all. Judging by her heavy breathing - her breasts were bellowing in and out - I could feel a rupture in the space/time continuum was abound unless Blake and his friend learnt the skillful art of humility and contrition within the next six seconds.

'Miss,' Blake shouted over the music, 'are you a lesbian?' His chum giggled as Blake winked and licked his lips at her, gasping for a response. He then elbowed his chuckling friend in the ribs. 'Shuddup Dre, you fuckin' paedo. Let the bitch speak.'

Rather than scream blue murder, Rachel's face contorted - her simmering anger summoning up a far more valuable life lesson. 'Blake, I'm not dignifying that with an answer.'

'So you are a fuckin' dyke!' Blake screamed insanely whilst coughing out a plume of smoke. 'Fuck man, Dre, look, she's not *dignitating* our answer with a question, it always means "yes". Do you finger yourself, Ms Weir?' Blake asked as he passed the joint to Dre.

'No I do not.'

Blake cackled wildly as Dre toked on the joint and passed it back.

'Miss, do you shave your pussy?' he asked, as he sucked down on the joint. Blake and Dre burst out laughing and fist bumped one another. Their hands barely made contact - they were that stoned.

I myself could barely process what I was seeing. I was shocked. Why wasn't Rachel karate-chopping these would-be serial killers down?

A gentle sobbing could be heard from one of the five cubicles. It was the only one of five that had the door locked shut - the farthest one along, right next to where Blake and Dre were idly floating and giggling. The sobbing got louder; there was clearly someone in there.

Blake jumped over to the cubicle and punched it with his fist. 'Shut the fuck up you little slut!'

The punching action sent his fist flying backward, nearly causing him to trip up over himself.

'Blake, you've done it now.' Rachel was taking no more BS, and marched right to the door and rattled it violently. She paused for a moment, and knocked on it three times.

'It's Ms Weir. Who's in there?'

'I'm not coming out,' said the little voice from inside the cubicle.

'Please, open up. It's okay.' The cackling interference of the walkie talkie wasn't helping matters, as it only aided to the sound of a potential crime scene which, I guess, this had become.

'Bye Miss! Love you!' Blake said, as he bent over and grabbed his belongings. His mate Dre did the same. They quickly swiped their trousers from the floor and bolted out of the toilets together, cackling all the way.

'Blake! Dre! Come back here!' screamed Rachel, as the door slammed shut behind them. I stepped forward, offering my assistance.

'Rachel, do you want me to—'

'—no, Joy. It's okay. We'll get them.' Rachel returned to the cubicle door. 'Sweetie, it's okay. You're not in trouble. Please open the door.'

The locking mechanism unbolted from inside and the door crept slowly open to reveal a soaking wet and shivering little girl. She was squatting completely in the nude by the toilet with her arms wrapped around her knees. She had been sobbing hard but appeared to have gotten over the worst of it. The image of this girl - it was hard to tell her age or what year she was in - shook my soul to the core.

'Oh my God.' I felt sick, and had to look away.

Rachel carefully squatted down to address her face to face. 'Ruby, sweetie. It's me, Ms. Weir. Are you okay?'

Ruby looked up and tried to smile, but to no avail. She did nod, albeit pathetically. 'What happened?' Rachel asked.

'They made me drink from the toilet.'

Rachel sighed, sympathetically. I'm guessing she was acting empathetic but, of course, I'd risk asserting that she may herself have been in a similar situation once. I'd never find out the answer to that particular question.

'Is that all they did?'

'Blake put his finger in me, Miss—'

'—Ruby, stop. You know I can't promise not to tell anyone else.'

My heart sunk. I stepped backward and covered my mouth. I think it was to stop my jaw from hitting the floor. For a moment I thought I was actually going to throw up. Rachel saw me doing all this and turned to face Ruby once again.

'They made me smoke the fag as well, Miss.'

'Ruby, look,' Rachel said, reassuringly, 'I'll need you to write a statement for me, okay? I have to inform CP. Please wait till then. Don't say anything else just now.'

'No! Don't tell anyone, Miss!' Ruby said, anxiously.

Rachel inspected Ruby's bloodshot eyes as she tried to step away. Ruby looked at me. I was a stranger. I certainly had no business being here, stripping further her right to privacy.

Rachel looked at me and tried for a smile. 'Miss, could you go to reception. Ask them to call the police and Child Protection and let them know I have Ruby Harwood in year eight.'

'Yes of course', I said, want to be anywhere but here right now.

I stepped out into the bright sunshine and was immediately dazzled by the broad daylight. I scanned around and immediately remembered where reception was, and turned the corner. It was a mere twenty or so footsteps from the reception area.

As I approached, I asked the receptionist to call the police.

'Who are you?'

'I'm, uh, here with Rachel. Ms Weir.'

'Why do you need the police?'

'There's been an incident in the girl's toilet in the annexe. Ms Weir is with a girl, I can't remember her name. But you need to call the police.'

'What happened?' snapped a voice from behind me. I turned around. It was Mr Martelle, the headmaster.

'Oh, we found a girl and a couple of lads in the toilet. They were smoking weed in there,' I said. Mr Martelle squinted his eyes at me and made for the annexe. I walked behind him.

'His name wasn't Harwood, by any chance?' he asked, as I caught up and walked with him.

'No, that's the girl's name. I think his name was Blake'.

Back in the girls toilets Ruby had managed to stand upright. Rachel had charitably removed her own over shirt and secured Ruby's modesty with it, wrapped around her midriff. Mr Martelle looked around, acknowledged the graffiti on the wall, and turned to Rachel.

'Blake again?' he snapped. Rachel closed her eyes and nodded her head. The weed haze was starting to overwhelm everyone. I could barely keep my stinging eyes open.

'Are you okay, Ruby?' Mr Martelle asked. She nodded yes. She was fine, after all. It was more of a shock than anything else.

'The police are coming. Sorry, I've forgotten your name?' Mr Martelle said to me.

The sound of the school alarm sounded off around us signaling the start of break time.

'Joy. Joy Attwood.'

'Excellent'

'Yes, *In Their Shoes*.'

'Oh no, not again. Is that where they've stashed their stuff? For goodness' sake,' Mr Martelle said, entirely misunderstanding what I had meant. 'Ruby, let's get you to welfare. We'll have to inform your parents and CP. Again.'

This news didn't go down terribly well with Ruby.

'No! Dad'll kill him!' Ruby screamed at the top of her lungs. Rachel leaned forward and held Ruby steady, trying to stop her from hurting herself. Ruby sobbed into Rachel's chest.

'I'm sorry, Ruby. We have to report it by law.'

'Blake left his phone in the sink. He'll be back,' Rachel said as she cradled the crying Ruby.

Mr. Martelle's attention was caught by the graffiti on the wall. 'Ms Weirdo is a Home-o?' Mr Martelle muttered to himself, perplexed. 'That doesn't even work?'

'Yeah,' Rachel quipped as she held the sobbing Ruby tighter against her chest, 'you can see the English classes are working.'

6

Reeespec' Mah Authoritay!

Rachel and I stared out of one of the windows in her classroom, observing the children in playground one storey below us. Her classroom had frosted, dulled glass on four of the windows by the computers, but the one we were looking out of in the other half of the room did not. It was totally transparent. I suppose this meant that if any of them looked up they'd see us looking down at them.

'It gives us a false sense of superiority, if you really want to read into the psychology of it,' mused Rachel as she stared down at the rabble. 'A sort of omnipresence.'

To the right of the playground two girls were eating a sandwich as they swung their legs. Next to them five boys were huddled together looking at something on a mobile phone.

Over the opposite side near the entrance to the reception some boys were filling up their empty water bottles from the fountain. They sprayed each other just as a teacher walked past and ordered them to stop.

'Sometimes I just like to people watch, you know?' said Rachel, leaning against the sill and popping open the window by its hinges. 'Look at all of them. Look at their behaviour. Future teachers. Doctors. Lawyers. Well, maybe not the last two,' she mused.

'It strikes me that you're not terribly fond of your students. Would that be a fair assessment?' I asked, feeling more encouraged to ask given the morning's trauma we'd been through.

Rachel coughed and wiped her lip with her sleeve. 'No, that's not true at all. It's just that, you know, given we're in the arse-end of Wiltshire and we're a grade three school…' she said, thinking aloud. 'Put it like this. If you give me eggs, I'll make you an omelette. You know?'

'Okay,' I responded, 'but don't the children deserve the opportunity to achieve at their fullest potential?'

Rachel glared at me and "harrumphed" to herself. 'You ever considered a career in education? You're beginning to sound just like him.'

As I thought about her remark, Rachel's attention was drawn across the room to David Bland's entrance. 'Speak of the devil,' she uttered to herself, before launching into pristine professional mode. David half-smiled and made himself at home at the nearest available table. He took extra care to sit down properly, and firmly; throwing out both arms to enable his sleeves to roll back up his wrists. He looked like he meant business.

'Please, Ms Weir, have a seat,' he said, as he pushed his glasses up the bridge of his nose and glanced attentively at his notes. David didn't acknowledge me and so I just sat down next to Rachel, opposite him. It felt like we were in the head teacher's office; two naughty little girls, about to get told off. At least, that was the vibe he was giving off.

'What's this about, David?'

'Well, Ms Weir—'

'Rachel.'

'Yea-huh, sure. Rachel, Mr Martelle received an email during period two from a student who was in your first period. A complaint.'

'What's it about?'

David took this moment to sigh and pause, for dramatic effect. One could argue he was enjoying the moment. All indicators pointed toward David being in control as he perused the email printout. He then looked at me, and took yet another dramatic breath and exhaled. 'Ms Altwild, I'm afraid this is confidential and so I'd ask you not to include this in your book if you wouldn't mind.'

'Sure,' I said. 'Not a problem at all. I'm changing everyone's name, including Beth's. So no need to worry.'

David closed his eyes and shook his head.

'Yea-huh sure. But it's just that if you were to change the name of the complainant, then you may change it to someone else's name - quite accidentally - and end up incriminating someone else at the school.'

Puzzled, I quickly arrived at a solution.

'Well, perhaps I could change it to a name of someone who's not at your school.'

'Like who?'

'I don't know. Maybe "Linda"?'

'No, we've six Lindas at Maxwell Gooder's. Three in year eight, and three in year nine,' he said.

'Okay, how about "Dawn"?'

'Yea-huh sure. We have six Dawns as well. Mmm.'

Rachel chimed in. 'So, the complainant is female?'

David's eyebrows raised. He thought quickly on his feet. 'Not necessarily, it could have been a boy.' It was quite convincing, but not enough to fool either me or Rachel.

'So who was it?' asked Rachel, grasping the moment to rile David up before he found his groove.

'I can't say while Joy's on the record.'

'But you won't let me change the name,' I said.

'How about you redact the name in your transcript?'

'Look, this section might not even make it to the final copy,' I said.

'I would rather you redact it or, if not, I'll have to ask you to leave the room. I'm afraid this is confidential information and her name cannot be revealed,' he said.

David bit his lip and realised his impersonal pronoun faux pas had let the sex of the 'complainant' slip. He quickly averted the mistake he'd just made. 'We'd rather not breach the Data Protection Act.'

'So it is a girl, then? That kinda narrows it down,' Rachel snapped and folded her arms.

'How about I use Poppy?' I asked. David's face suggested there are more than one Poppy at the school.

'No, we have seven Poppys.'

'Lolita, then?'

'Are you mad? In a school?' barked David, clearly getting agitated. There was an awkward silence as Rachel smiled at my working on David's integrity. She was right, there was an unearthly false modesty about him that needed dismantling. It was starting to irritate even me.

'You are DBS checked, aren't you?' he asked me, threateningly.

'Yes,' I lied. 'How about Shani'qua?'

David scowled at me through his inordinate and perfectly round spectacles, indicating he was becoming increasingly fed up with this exchange. 'Redact the name. Please. Or I'll have to ask you to leave.'

'Fine. I'll blank the name out.'

'Yea-huh sure. Many thanks.' David adjusted his tie and cleared his throat. 'Is it true that you used the F word in class, period one?'

'No. I didn't,' Rachel insisted. She was very convincing as we both knew she was guilty as hell.

'Did you refer to anyone in the class as "sarcastic"?'

'What does that even mean?'

'I suppose what I'm trying to ascertain is whether or not you are using your advanced literary lexicon to disparage the less-educated pupils in your care.'

'In English, please!'

'The accusation is that you said the F word to--'

'Which I didn't—'

'--and that you attacked the person in question, accusing her of being quote-unquote, thick.'

'I didn't.'

An awkward pause. Rachel bit her bottom lip, which

caused David to squint his eyes at her. He slid the email printout in front of Rachel. 'Are you saying this student is lying?'

Rachel scanned the paper as she drew it to her gaze by her forefinger. She read it carefully.

For clarity, what follows is a necessarily redacted transcript (verbatim) between Ms Rachel Weir and Mr David Bland.

Rachel Weir: She's lying. None of that happened.

David Bland: Yea-huh, sure. So, just to clarify, are you saying that ▮▮▮ is lying?

RW: Yes, I am. And it's not the first time ▮▮▮▮ 's lied, either. Her and that cretinous friend of hers, ▮▮▮▮ - do you remember the trouble those two caused during the Cheddar Gorge field trip? ▮▮▮ and her father threatened to sue the school over that 'injury' she 'sustained', before we discovered it was all a put-on?

DB: A number of others in the class have verified ▮▮▮ 's story, too.

RW: Who.

DB: ▮▮▮ and ▮▮▮▮▮ both said you had used the F-word, as well as personally attacked ▮▮▮ by calling her sarcastic.

RW: Since when was it a crime to call anyone 'sarcastic'? I suppose if you removed the 'a', 'r' and 'c' and replaced it with a 'p', you might be on to something.

DB: You full well know who ▮▮▮ 's parents are. Surely you understand that I am duty-bound to follow this up. Mr Martelle demands it. I have to report back to him and, hopefully, stop all this from escalating. Especially when it comes from a HOT student.

RW: Oh! Right! Now it all makes sense. I see why you're being a ██ about this. Just because ██ 's dad is a QC and her mum is on the board of governors.

DB: That's got nothing to do with it.

RW: What about that outright lie she told last term about Mrs. Prendergast doing a line of ██████ out of her desk drawer during that study skills period. ██ 's a bloody liability. Thank God we have unions when there are vile, vindictive ███s like ██ around.

DB: ██ owned up and apologised for the Prendergast misunderstanding. She was going through a tough time.

RW: Prenders got suspended!

DB: Yes, on full pay! While the investigation was ongoing!

RW: The woman nearly lost her job! ██ is a proven liability and has an abysmal track record for veracity. She may well be classed as a Higher Order Thinker by the school, and I agree - it's certainly true when it comes to her ability to tell tall tales.

DB: Regardless, the fact that ██ 's mother is on the board of governors is not pertinent to this line of enquiry, I can assure you.

RW: Why are you taking ██ 's side, David, tell me? You got an axe to grind? Did I do something to upset or offend you?

DB: I'm not siding with anyone. I'm doing my job!

RW: This accusatory tone of yours. I knew I should have gone to the union about this.

DB: She's off sick today, and this incident demands immediate attention. Look, Rachel, I'm not accusing you of anything. I'm merely gathering the facts.

RW: Right, and how's that going for you? What facts have you gleaned so far, huh, David? Apart from the fact you're overreacting and have reached judgement before getting both sides of the story?

DB: Please don't be defensive about this. I'm just doing my job.

RW: Yeah, you said that already. You're such a ██████ing ███████ sometimes, you know. You're not winning many friends around here, I can tell you.

DB: I can see you're angry. Please, let's start from the beginning.

RW: ████ you, David.

DB: Right. Start again. For the record, so I can take this back to Mr Martelle. Are you categorically refuting this allegation?

RW: Yes. Emphatically.

DB: But

RW: No.

~ Transcript ends ~

Rachel and I found ourselves once again in her "main office" - the smoking area. This time, I noticed a wheelie bin three-quarters full of cigarette butts, empty fag packets and used milkshake bottles. Clearly this bin hadn't been emptied since Anthony Eden's day.

'I can't wait till today's over. I just wanna go home and sleep.' Rachel was on her second cigarette of the session, brushing the dry coffee stains from her shirt and contemplating her life.

'Only four more days 'till half term!' said another woman, approaching us, sparking up a cigarette.

'Oh, Hi Josie,' said Rachel. 'Winning?'

Josie was in her forties and had a quasi-Bohemian look to her. She nodded her head dramatically and smiled. 'Yeah. Only four more hours to go until home time!'

Rachel introduced us. Josie was second in the science department, excluding chemistry. Chemistry, I was told, had its own department due to the complexity of its material, in much the same way that English and Business didn't. Those two departments had converged two years ago. To me, this made absolutely no sense.

'Decisions at this school rarely make sense, but you just have to go with the decisions of SMT,' Josie, chuckled.

'What's SMT?' I asked.

'Senior Moment Team,' Josie said, flippantly. 'Nah, they're the management - you know, the head teacher, the assistant head and deputy, et cetera.'

'I see,' I said, contemplatively. 'So what does 'second' in the department actually mean?'

Josie thought about the question.

'I've absolutely no idea. I should really find out one of these days.'

We stood smiling at one another as Rachel took another drag of her smoke. 'Oh, while I remember. Raych, do you teach Isla Jagger, year nine?'.

'Yes,' Rachel said. 'Why?

'Well, apparently she's in a huff about a teacher calling her names. Rumour is that she called her a "spastic". Can you believe that? In this day and age, with the economy and job market the way it is, some idiot goes and does that! Tch!'

'Yeah. It was me,' said Rachel, ostentatiously. 'And it wasn't "spastic". It was *sarcastic*.'

'Sarcastic or not, calling her a spastic was a bold move,' Josie said.

'I never said "spastic",' Rachel sighed, becoming irritable. 'Oh what does it matter.'

Josie looked shocked. 'I actually kinda admire that, you know. In a perverse way.'

Rachel raised her eyebrows and took another drag from her cigarette. She casually flicked the ash away from her, directly onto my shoes, and stared at the trees in the opposite direction.

'So Josie, have you been teaching here long?' I asked, trying to break the awkwardness.

'Nearly four years,' she replied as she playfully tapped Rachel's shoulder. 'Oh, Raych, I just had the sweetest year eights just now. Super-well behaved. An absolute dream. We did enzymes and they just, you know, got right on with it, not a peep,' said Josie.

Rachel wasn't sharing the riotously good mood Josie found herself in. In this job, it's clear that there are good days and bad days - and for Josie, it was the former. For Rachel? Far too early to say, as she chugged hungrily on her cigarette.

'Caught Blake with Ruby in the toilets again during on-call,' Rachel said, the colour in her face starting to drain.

'Oh for goodness' sake. Again?' Josie snapped, struggling to contain her disgust. 'Has someone informed Dad yet?'

'Dunno,' Rachel said as she shrugged her shoulders and flicked more cigarette ash to the floor. 'And then if that wasn't boring enough, I had Bland exert his suck-upphancy on me.'

'Oh, that lanky grey streak of boring piss. What did he want?'

'The stupid complaint.'

I stood absolutely speechless as I took in what I was hearing. One imagines the most noble profession in the world might include reverence and respect for one another. Particularly authority. It was certainly true in the corridors and staff rooms within the building.

Out there in the quiet, modestly-removed environment of the perpetual chain-smoker a bizarre logic and brutal truth was at work. These teachers were behaving like their students - speaking explicitly about their managers like students talk about their teachers.

I feel as if I've illegally acquired the cheat codes into what teachers really think.

'Jesus, Bland is such a boring bastard,' said Josie. 'What is it about people called 'David'? They're just so tedious. Honestly, that four-eyed, thin-on-top twat could bore for Europe.' Josie said, as she adjusted her own glasses. Rachel giggled at Josie's deprecating remark, and started to lighten up a bit. She rolled her shoulders.

'Yeah, and guys called Patrick are almost always Irish. You ever notice that?' Rachel contributed, as Josie laughed and playfully patted Rachel's shoulder once again.

'Is he really as bad as he appears?' I ask, seeing as we're in the mode of truth telling.

'Who, Bland? Right-Hand Bland Shandy? He's right out of a Dickens novel, he is. Right down to his surname,' Josie sniggered with utter contempt for the subject of her diatribe. 'He belongs in a school along with Mr Shouty, Mrs Wet and Mr Skive-Off-For-Three-Months-With-Occupational-Stress.'

Josie clearly believed everything she had just said. 'Honestly, the man is a dullard. He accosted me the other day for having an open tin of fizzy drink on my desk. You should have seen the look on his face in front of 10Gx when I told him it was being used as part of an experiment on Amino acids. He thought it was for my own personal use,' Josie chuckled, the rasp of her tar-stained lungs fighting to catch air.

Another woman emerged from behind Josie and Rachel; a lady in her early sixties - small in stature, but very energetic for her age. 'Hi guys,' she said. 'Ohh, you're new here. I'm Gloria. Nice to meet you.'

'Hi, I'm Joy. I'm doing a documentary on Rachel.'

'Ooh, very nice. I'm just the cover, so don't mind me!' Gloria said, taking out a cigarette.

'Heavy day?' asked Josie.

'Nah, cover's been all right, actually,' said Gloria as she struck a match and lit her cigarette. 'Only two off sick, and another two on a field trip, but - yeah - we're okay. We'll get through it.'

Gloria took the first draw from her cigarette. 'As I say, only four more days till half term, and bingo!' Gloria over-exaggerated a shudder - giddy at the prospect of a whole week off work. 'You okay, Raych, honey?'

'Yeah, I'm okay. Just, you know, one thing after another.' Rachel violently flicked the hot cherry off the end of her cigarette, and chucked the butt in the bin. 'Shot!' Rachel exclaimed - a pathetically microscopic victory in an otherwise utterly depressing day for her so far.

'We'd better go, guys. Joy is teaching her first ever class in five minutes!' Rachel said to the other two.

Oh shit. She's right. I'd forgotten about that. I was meant to be teaching period three!

In the hectic circus of the day's events, both Rachel and I must have parked it at the back of our minds as we'd dealt with all the commotion from the morning.

I suddenly felt very, very sick. My palms begans to sweat. Could Rachel, Josie and Gloria tell? No, thank God. I'd learnt fairly early on today that if I were to survive being a teacher - even for eighty minutes - I'd need to be thick-skinned and put on an act. The students would eat me up, otherwise.

'Good luck!' Josie encouraged, as Rachel and I made our departure.

We were back in Rachel's classroom. She flicked through a text book. I paced around, riddled with anxiety and was trying my best not to hyperventilate.

'Okay, I got it. It's "Lateral Thinking". You're okay with that, right?'

'Yes, I think so. That's where you have … uh, like Schrödinger's Cat, isn't it? Is it dead or is it alive?'

'No, not quite. But you're in the right ball park,' said Rachel, as she scanned the book. Her remarkable brain was deciphering the words to make the content more palatable for my green ears. Maybe one day I'd become this experienced too. 'It's basically what the creatively-challenged in this school refer to as "Blue Sky Thinking".'

'They're teaching this in English, now?' I asked.

'Actually this is a Business class.'

'I have to teach the kids to think laterally?'

'It's easy,' snapped Rachel, quick-thinking as she snatched a random example seemingly out of thin air. 'For example, a captain is on the ocean and gets a message saying that the Captain's husband had died. How can this possibly be?' she asked. 'Think, come on. Think laterally.'

'He's gay?' I offered, knowing I was wrong. 'Ugh, no,' I thought, as my mind was elsewhere repeating the word 'ocean', over and over, hoping it'd commit itself to memory. 'He's dead!'

'No! It's a woman! The captain of the boat is a woman! It's like debunking one's prejudice. We're conditioned to think a certain way, but when we think laterally—'

'—oh Raych, look, I don't know if I can do this. Maybe you should just do it. It's okay, I can just pretend I did it - none of the readers will know, anyway. I'll tell Andrew to just make it up.'

'Oi, Altwild!' Rachel snapped.

'Attwood—'

'—like it matters' she interrupted, seeming to take great offense to my bottling-out. 'You're not *not* doing this, you understand? You're documenting me and my Godforsaken profession. Don't you show me up! Don't you dare bail out on me now. You're scared? I got news for you. Everyone's scared. Now, grow some fucking ladybollocks and smash it. Okay?'

Rachel was one hell of a motivator. She seemed very offended by my proposal to back out at the last minute. But in my own defence, I had nothing prepared. Did it matter? Was this really what teaching was like? Do teachers just fly by the seat of their pants like this? Surely not. Oh God, what if the students laugh at me? Or I can't get them to shut up and listen?

'Please tell me they're a nice bunch, at least.'

Rachel paused, in a way that suggested that she could lie. 'Sure, they're a lovely bunch of year eights. Twelve year-olds. Piece of cake.'

The school buzzer blared and echoed thunderously around the corridors, laughing and pointing at me as I entered a frenzy of nerves and sphincter-winking.

I paced around muttering the word "cake" over and over, mixed with the occasional utterance of the word "ocean".

'Of course, it's perfect,' Rachel realised. She dived over to the computer keyboard and acted on her private, sudden epiphany.

I slapped my forehead and grabbed a white board pen from the holder underneath the board and twiddled it between my fingers. I remembered now why I used to smoke, and regretted quitting now more than ever. 'Cake, Ocean, Ocean, Cake', I muttered quickly, as Rachel typed something into YouTube's search facility.

'Can I quickly go to the toilet before we start?'

The thunderous arrival of child-like screaming, pushing

and shouting from behind the door answered my question before Rachel had the chance to.

I turned, slowly, to face the door. It vibrated - actually, breathed before my eyes - as it was banged from the outside by the flailing arms and other appendages of the kids jacked up on a sugar high from break who were awaiting their class. 'Oh no,' I muttered to myself. I turned to Rachel, and bit my lip.

'Time to get tough, sweetie,' she said, chuckling. She seemed to be enjoying my nervousness. I guess she must have been here before, too. 'En-joy yourself!'

The music started to play. The first two lyrics of the track happened to be the last two words I uttered to myself not eight seconds ago. The track is *Cake by the Ocean* by DNCE, and I'd rather be drowning in one than standing here right now. An ocean, I mean. Not cake.

I was about to teach my first ever class.

7
The JOY of S.E.X
(Secondary Education
eXperience)

I opened the door, and mimicked what I had seen Rachel do during her first period; I leaned against the door, propping it open and eyed the messy line of students who snaked messily up against the wall. One of them was playing with a piece of canvas art by moving its position left and right. Two students waved their ties around.

It suddenly made complete sense that the well-behaved kids were at the front of the line; the not-so-well-intentioned kids were in the middle, and the outright animals were at the back.

Most everyone in the queue eventually stopped what they were doing and stared right at me, presumably wondering where Ms Weir was. I was a strange face, in a strange town; my unfamiliar face meant I could be anyone.

I could in actual fact be anyone. It may work to my advantage. For the common student, "anyone" might mean an external authority figure; maybe I'm from another school? Might I be a supply teacher? I decided to say nothing. Just at that moment, the Joy I've known for the past twenty-odd years vanished, and was replaced by another Joy. An angry Joy.

'Okay,' I barked, imitating my best impression of the drill sergeant from *Full Metal Jacket*. 'Guys, settle down and line up!' They did as instructed. I couldn't get the image of the drill instructor out of my head. My hands were shaking.

'You two, at the back. Where are your ties?' I shouted. They looked back, apologetic, and held up their ties up as their answer. 'Yes, those are ties. Well done. Why aren't they around your necks?' They quickly clipped them to their collar. 'Thank you.'

It worked. I had set a dangerous precedent for the rest of the period. If I didn't keep this stern act up for this period I knew they were going to have their way with me.

I peered down at the boy who was messing around with the canvas art, and surprised him with an evil glance. He took the message, chewed his lip apologetically, and adjusted it perfectly against the wall. It made me smile. He probably thought I was smiling as a result of his contrition. Little did he know that my smile was the result of my 'act' working.

'Okay, in you go,' I said, standing back and waving them in.

They filtered in very calmly and headed for their seats. I watched on, trying to swallow back my utter terror. My hands started shaking, and it was only a matter of time before this became visible. So, I put them behind the small of my back and clasp one hand over the other, appearing relaxed. I suddenly felt like a teacher.

To aid my relaxation, I was glad that the song Rachel had started was having a positive effect on the kids; they knew - and liked - *Cake by the Ocean*, and even though they were on their best behaviour, it was easy to spot the slight bopping of the heads to the tune as the first ones in took their seats. I held back my amusement by remaining stony silent and keeping my mouth straight.

I removed my foot from the door and approached the white board.

As the music flew around the room, it acted as a sort of

perverse soundtrack to what I genuinely believed was about to be one the most embarrassing and soul-crushing experiences of my life. I'd always seen teachers on TV and in movies and thought "Meh, how hard could that be? I could do that much better!"

I mean, how many times have any of us have sat through - or rather, suffered - a presentation at work, miring over how we could have done it better; to capture the audience's attention and engage them better than the dolt we're trying to stay awake for?

For possibly the third time in my life, beside sitting my GCSEs and my recent marriage, I heard whatever arrogance I knew existed within me getting stabbed to death by a crazy person with a machete. It may sound overly melodramatic here, but - as the last pair of buttocks took their seat - "Joy" died, and was reborn.

SCH-TOMPP!! The door slammed shut. I jumped. The hinges must have worn down.

'Jesus Christ!' I exclaimed. The kids laughed at this retort, as I walked in front of the white board.

'Ha. Miss, the door is broken. It does that all the time!' said a boy to my right. He giggled. I glanced briefly at Rachel who was at the back of the room.

She looked up, smiled, and nodded at me. I'm sure she meant it with encouragement, but I couldn't help but feel that it had a "see how you like this" feel to it as she winked at me and licked her lips.

'Miss,' asked a girl in the front row. 'What's your name?'

I froze. What was bloody my name!? It begins with a J — but, no, not in this class it doesn't. It begins with an "A". I bought myself some time. 'Have a guess,' I blurted, my mouth sixteen steps ahead of my brain. The girl thought and quickly responded. 'Is it Miss Smith?' she said, quite innocently. The others chuckled, which in turn prompted around five little hands firing into the air, all keen to take their guess.

'No. No it's not.' I was buying myself time, and looked

at another hand. 'Yes?'

'Is it Miss Nervous?' the boy chuckled.

'No.' "And fuck you, too" I thought. Thankfully it didn't escape my lips.

Almost every one of the twenty students put their hand in the air, eager to have a go. I shook my head and smiled. Rachel giggled to herself as she looked down to mark some work. I had an epiphany and lifted my head. I don't know where it came from, but I turned to the board and drew seven small lines for my surname on it, spun around and said 'Hangman!'

The children's faces all lit up, excited. I pointed at the right-most kid on the first table. 'Gimme a letter?' I asked - my white board marker poised at the board.

'S,' said the boy.

'Nope,' I said, as I wrote the letter underneath the lines and drew the spine of the gallows. I went to the next kid and raised my eyebrows.

'Er... 'A'?!'

'Yes, good!' I replied, as I filled in the first line with an 'A'. Every kid squealed with delight.

On to the next kid. 'A letter, please?' The kid searched his memory bank for a letter, but took his time, prompting the others to get shifty and impatient.

'Erm, erm...' muttered the boy, as the kid next to him nudged his arm.

'A letter, dick head!' he said.

'I'm thinking! Erm... Z? He offered. I smirked and wrote "Z" next to the "S", and drew the base of the gallows. 'Aww shit!' said the boy.

'Language!' I said, sternly, as I looked at the next girl. She smiled and bowed her head in embarrassment.

'P?' she said. Another voice barked out from the opposite end of the room.

'We already had 'P' you idiot!' I shot the owner of that voice - a puffy-jawed cherub with freckles - a nasty look. 'Oh and you're *not* an idiot are you, genius?' I snapped, sending a wave of 'Oooohs' and 'Aaaaahs' - followed by a wave of laughter - among his nearest peers.

I felt the bully in me rise up out of my abdomen. I puffed out my chest. 'You like calling people an idiot, do you? What's your name?' I asked, slipping on my metaphorical boxer gloves.

'Adam.'.

'Adam. Nice one. The first human being constructed by God, ' I rattled, hoping for a laugh. 'So you're bound to get a letter right, aren't you? Gimme a letter.' Adam screwed his face.

'R', he said. I smirked and acted as if he was right, sending his ego into the stratosphere - only to drop it from a great height. I quickly scribbled "R" under into the 'incorrect' area. As I did this, the class erupted and laughed, thumping the tables.

Adam's humiliation did two things; A) asserted my authority, and B) sent a message out that I didn't suffer nonsense easily. I realise of course that the phrase is "don't suffer fools gladly" but I was quickly realising that with twenty children in a room, at least three of them were statistically bound to be genuine idiots.

I looked at Adam as his face fell. 'Wrong!' I said, as I moved to his neighbour.

'T,' said the neighbour.

'Good!' I said, writing down the two Ts of my name. Only four letters remained undiscovered. A girl sitting right in front of me seemed to have arrived at a complete answer. Insistently, she threw her hand into the air. Such was her insistence, that I broke consistency and looked at her. 'Miss, is the next letter 'W'? She asked.

'Yes it is, well done,' I said, writing the "W" onto the fourth line.

'I think I know what it is, then.'

'Go on, then.'

'It's Altwild.'

'Ah, no.' My stupid visitor badge! Derisory laughs and

general disdain for the girl jumped around the room. I took this insult as a direct attack on me (erroneously) and slammed the pen against the white board.

'Be quiet!' I barked. 'But there is a 'W' in it, so well done,' I said to her as I wrote the 'W' on the fourth line. 'Okay,' I said, wanting to speed the process up, 'can anyone guess what the rest of my name *wood* be? Anyone, what *wood* it be?' I asked, emphasising a certain word. The psychology clearly worked.

'It's Attwood!' exclaimed the "genius" kid, Adam.

'Bingo!' I said, to his surprise.

'Is it actually?'

'Yes! You really are infallible. Just like your Dad!' I wrote out my surname fully on the hangman lines. Some of the kids laughed, and others sighed as they hadn't been afforded their shot. 'Attwood!' screamed half of the voices in the class. 'You got it,' I smiled, stepping into my mental teacher overalls as the nerves evaporated from my stomach.

I turned around and glared at the half-drawn gallows and swiped a massive 'Z' right through it with my pen, like Zorro marking his territory.

'Okay,' I announced, 'here's a question for you. A man rides into a town on Monday, and leaves on a Tuesday. But he only spent ten minutes in the town. How can this be?'

The faces stared back at me in puzzlement.

'What?' said a voice from the back table. Another hand shot up into the air, eager to answer.

'Yes?' I asked.

'Because he arrived at five minutes to midnight?' said a boy with spectacles and fuzzy hair.

'No, that's not the right answer. But that was a very good guess,' I said. Actually, the boy was technically correct. It was clear he possessed the way of thinking required to nail this particular topic.

'The man's watch is broken and he's confused,' said

another voice. 'No,' I replied.

'Is it a trick question, Miss?' posed another.

'No, it's not a trick question. Think about it,' I instructed. 'How can a man arrive somewhere on Monday?' Still no signs of life, although most were looking around searching for the answer. Two boys at the back became impatient and started elbowing each other at the middle table, and agitating one another. 'What are you two doing?'

'He's hitting me!'

'Just stop it. Think of the answer.'

As they continued to think, I scanned the room. I absorbed each of their faces and suddenly remembered what life had been like for me in classes at school. I spent most of my time trying to be as diligent and hardworking as possible, but I fail to recall sitting in a class like this, having to think laterally. School has come a long way since I'd been attending it.

'Okay,' I said. 'Maybe it's time for a clue. When you think of the word 'Monday' what do you think of?' The faces then started to search for the answer. Then - as if on cue - the mental prompt evidently began to work. A girl at the far back, sitting near Rachel, put her hand up instantly.

'Yes?' I asked her.

'Is Monday the name of car he drives?' she asked.

'Yes, it is!' I exclaimed. 'Actually it's his horse, and not a car. But I'll accept it. Well done!'

A light flashed on inside me. The girl looked extremely pleased with herself, as the others groaned and muttered something along the lines of "I knew that!" to themselves. The look on the girl's face made it all worthwhile. She'd genuinely achieved something.

The groans quickly turned to chuckles.

'Miss, what's this got to do with business?' asked another girl. Good question. What does this have to do with business studies. Thinking laterally? I paused to look at Rachel; my somewhat remote confidant. She didn't look up at me as she was too busy with her marking. I was stranded and alone. I had to think of something. So, I just gave in to my instincts.

'What do you think it has to do with business?' I asked the girl, buying myself some time. The girl pondered this question, taking on the challenge.

'So we see questions a different way?', she replied, slightly anxious that she might be wrong.

'Yes!' I said, secretly thanking her for the germ of an excuse that I now fully intended to exploit. 'That's correct,' I said, not knowing how the rest of my sentence would go. 'It is about thinking differently. Thinking laterally. That's how some of the best ideas happen!' I said, searching the room for an example.

My eyes settled on a Fun-Tastic Fact-Toidz poster on the far wall. I didn't have time to read it fully, but the protruding logo - a purplish, blue square with a white 'f' inside it - screamed out at me.

'Like, for example, the guy who invented FaceBook. Do you all know FaceBook?' I asked, hoping they'd say yes. My prayers were answered; they knew the example.

'Yeah, Adam's got naked selfies of his sister on there!' a boy to my right announced, heartily. Everyone laughed. I looked to Adam, as he stood up.

'Yeah, but at least my Dad's dick ain't on there like yours is!' Adam retorted.

'Seriously, look at his FaceBook page, Miss! His Dad's got a well small dick!' said Adam, proving himself to be quite the quick-witted comedian. I was about to call him Private Joker, but thought better of it and remained quiet. Besides, none of these twerps would have seen *Full Metal Jacket*, anyway. That said, I was impressed by the speed and relative wit of his response. Adam could surely win most arguments.

'Well I hope you don't take after your Dad, Adam!' I said, realising I had overstepped the line as the final word escaped my lips. I was overcome with shock and fear.

Teacher's wouldn't dare have said *that*. I didn't even know what I meant by saying it. And why are the kids now laughing as if that was the most hilarious thing they'd ever heard?

I realised anyone else could have taken this retort a number of ways. I sincerely meant it to mean "If that's true, then learn from your father's mistake and don't repeat it."

I now realise that - due to their laughter - I have implied that Adam and his father have small penises.

'God! No, no, I didn't mean it like that!' I implored to Adam. 'I meant, you should always—'

'Aha, Miss Attwood said you've got a small dick!' screamed another voice.

'No, I didn't!' I begged, waving my hands in front of the hail of verbal abuse now being fired at Adam, as he slumped down, defeated. The cackling chaos was now overwhelming the scene. As I looked down, I made eye contact inadvertently with a young Asian girl who smiled back at me. She had the sense not to join in the chanting of 'Small Dick! Small Dick!' with the others.

'Okay, be quiet! Enough!' I screeched, trying to abate the chaos. It didn't work. So I slammed the white board marker against the board itself three times. It got their attention. 'Oh. Have I got your attention now?' I asked, sternly. 'Now look, my point was that—'

'Miss, are you married?' a girl asked, interrupting my stride.

'Yes, I am.'

'Are you actually?'

'Yes.'

'What's his name?'

I nearly answered. But, bless this little girl, she actually gave me a gift. Quick thinking, I placed my hands on my hips and launched into a question that would ignite their lateral thinking prowess, challenge their prejudice and get them closer to me in the same go.

'What's your name?' I asked her.

'Felicity Harwood'.

The name seemed familiar. Harwood. 'Do you have an older brother at this school by any chance?'

Felicity nodded 'Yes, his name is Blake. He's in year eleven. Why, do you know him?'

'No, no, no…' I snapped, exploiting the opportunity to not bring up her elder sibling's attempted sexual assault from this morning. 'It's just that you look familiar. Ah, no matter!' I said. Phew. 'Okay, guess my other half's name.'

Veering quickly away from the topic of statutory rape was a good idea, I thought. But was asking this new question to avoid it a wise move? I literally had no time to think it through, but it felt like a good idea, and - as my retort to Adam proved two minutes ago - acting on instincts evidently produces one of two outcomes; overwhelming success, or irrevocable damage.

Felicity pondered on what the name of my other half might be.

Dear reader, for clarity, I should pause now to reveal that I am in a same-sex marriage. My wife's name is Jay. We've been married for nearly two years. Whenever I'm asked the name of 'my partner' - as I refer to her in polite society, due mainly to its ambiguity - people are satisfied with the answer 'Jay', taking it to mean a man, and then move on with their lives. I admit, I don't exactly make a point of her being a woman. After all, Jay could be short for Jason, Jerome or Jared. Actually, no. Not Jared (let's not go down that road.) But you get the idea.

I have used Jay's name as a benchmark - in some cases - as to whether or not people genuinely give a toss about me and my personal life; those who go on, one way or another, to discover that Jay is female confirms that they care enough to get to know me. If they don't, then it means that they either don't care or that the question was used just to fill time. Or both.

Those interactions till now have been with fully grown adults, capable of rational - if not lateral - thought. How would all this rub off on these children? I began regretting walking down this path, as I had no idea where it'd end up taking us.

'James?' said Felicity.

James - 'J' - my heart for a brief moment nearly stopped.

'Ah, no.'

'Are you doing parent's evening tonight, Miss?' a boy named Danny, said.

'No,' I replied. His face lit up - he was "in".

'So you're free tonight, Miss?' Danny said, licking his lips and winking at me. Unimpressed (although flattered, I suppose), I ignored him.

'Is it Edward?' a boy asked.

'No, it's not,' I replied. 'What's your name?'

'Edward,' said Edward.

I giggled; now that is how you charm a lady. 'That's very kind of you. Anyone else?' I asked, knowing how well the hangman game went down.

A bullet-storm of names ranging from the expected (Frank, Lee and Gerald) to the downright bizarre (Domingo, Leroy and, rather presciently, 'Kodak') headed my way. I must have heard scores of names - all male, most uninspired - before waving my hands for them to stop.

'Please, stop shouting random names at me. You'll never guess it.' I said. They stopped. They heard my last sentence perfectly well, but I may as well have said 'Okay here's the answer 3, 2, 1...', judging by their petulant, excited faces as they awaited my answer.

'It's Jay,' I said.

They seemed quite happy with that answer. 'What's "J" short for, Miss?' asked another child.

'It's not short for anything. It's Jay. J-A-Y,' I said. Again, they seemed fairly content with this answer. But contentedness never lasts so long as a child's brain is processing information, as I was about to discover.

'Is he a teacher, too, Miss?' Felicity asked.

'Well, I'm not a teacher,' I said, surprised by my sentence's ability to redirect the conversation away from my marriage.

'You're teaching now.'

'Yes, but this is only for a book I'm writing.'

'You write books?' said another voice.

'Yes. Sort of.'

'What kind of books?' said a tiny, female voice. I turned to look at her. 'Hello. What's your name?

'Paige Turner, Miss.' She said. I giggled. "Page Turner". How very droll. And quite apt, given the topic.

'Well, Paige, sweetie,' I said, the brooding maternal juices sizzling inside me. 'They're like documentaries where I spend a day with someone at their job so the reader can understand what a particular job is like. But it's for books.'

'Ugh, sounds boring.' Paige replied.

I glanced over at Rachel who had paused her marking, and was looking at me forlornly with her head in the palm of her hand. Not literally, of course, like a headless horseman; rather, her chin was resting on her palm and she was taking an interest in what I had just said.

'So what does he do?' asked a random mouth.

'Jay is a she,' I blurted out, still focusing on Rachel.

Rachel blinked and smiled and returned to her marking. Bugger. I'd let it slip. All that hard work, and I fall at the most stupid of hurdles. I was on my own with this one now.

'Your wife is a girl?' Felicity asked, stunned.

'Yes. Aren't most wives girls?'

'But you are a girl as well.'

'That means you're gay, Miss!' Adam snapped, as if he'd just this second discovered Penicillin and the untold fortunes it would bring. With that, a jeer of disapproval Mexican-waved its tedious, inexorable march from Adam to the other side of the room. They were now enemies of mine. Especially Paige Turner. The little shit. You can attack my sexual proclivities but to purposefully lance my new career in this way? Bitch. At least I don't have a stupid-sounding name! Ner-ner!

'Yes. I am gay. So what? Who gives a toss?' I said, placing my hands on my hips. The kids muttered to each other in precisely the same way I'd experienced when I came out to my friends five years ago.

Adam extended his arm to ask a question. 'Yes, Adam?' I asked, entirely defensively.

'So are you lesbian, Miss?' he said. I'd never been asked that question quite so directly before in my life.

'Yes, I am *a* lesbian. I am *one* lesbian.'

'That's peak, Miss!' Adam seemed delighted. I wasn't expecting that. 'Your videos on the internet are sick!' Adam finished, laughing with his friends. I think he even fist-bumped one or two of them. That'll teach me to speak before thinking. Hold on, what did he mean by saying they're *sick*?

'Lesbianism isn't a sickness, Adam,' I tried. 'It's a perfectly normal—'

'—no, Miss,' Adam explained, 'sick doesn't mean, like, being ill.'

'So what does it mean?'

'It means when something's really good. Like really, really good. "That's sick!"' Okay, I'm confused, now. I think I know what "Cowabunga" and "Cool" mean. Oh, who cares. I'm only here for a day, I thought. But I refused to let this gay nest of vipers go.

'Does anyone here have a problem with me being gay? Put your hands up.' Nothing. Absolute silence. 'No, really, don't be shy. I won't be angry. Put your hands up if it's a problem,' I said, seething inside.

My seething turned into apoplexy as six hands cautiously, and naively, climbed into the air. I was brave enough to withstand this response. If I could handle all the abuse on Twitter and FaceBook about my sexuality with people you'd think ought to know better, then surely I can challenge (at least) six misconceptions of immature minds. Besides, maybe this is something the others need to hear, as well.

'Okay, hands down,' I said. The hands went down as slowly as they rose. 'Here's a question for you. How many gay people do you know?' I asked, expecting the answer 'none'.

'None!' screamed a voice.

'Eurgh, no! No-one!' said another.

'My Uncle is gay,' said a girl in the front row, who, till now had been silent.

'Is he?' I said, 'What's your name?'

'Donna, Miss. He's in prison, as well.'

A light chuckling came from the other side of the room.

'What did he do?'

'He violated his parole, and they put him back inside,' was Donna's response.

Here's a question for you, dear reader. Let's say you were in my position. What do you do with information like that? Where can you go? And also, what gives you the right to have acquired that information in the first place? Nineteen other human beings you are about to share the rest of your school life with now know you have a family member who's gay and in prison. I felt extremely guilty, and no amount of instinct was going to lift me out of this situation. God alone knows what punchlines some of the mischievous class members were cooking up in their immature minds.

'It's okay, Miss. Everyone at school knows,' Donna said, rescuing me from my internal moral quagmire.

'My point,' I resumed to the class, 'is that each and every one of you here knows someone who's gay.'

'Well I don't!' said a boy.

'Yeah, me neither! That's sick!' said another.

'You mean "sick" as in "good?"' I asked, flippantly.

'No. Like disgusting.'

'For Heaven's sake, make your mind up!' I snapped. 'How do you know you don't know someone who's gay? You think every gay person goes around announcing it to everyone they know? How do you know?' I struggled to acclimatise my thoughts to that of a twelve year-old. I was failing quickly. I foolishly grasped a theoretical situation out of thin air.

'How do you know Ms Weir isn't gay?' I snapped, closing my eyes, realising what I'd just let myself in for. Sigh. Here we go…

'Is Ms Weir gay?' Adam asked.

'No, I mean—'

'—Ahaaa! Weirdo's a Homo!' shouted Adam.

A childish chorus of hysterical elation filled the room. I looked over, still gobsmacked, at Rachel who quickly looked down to avoid revealing how she truly felt. Needing to immediately rescue the situation, I slammed the white board marker against the white board three times. 'Ms Weir is not gay!'

'But you said she was!'

'No I did not. I asked you how you knew she wasn't.'

'What?'

'There's a difference.'

'Between what?'

'Look, it doesn't matter. Here's a question for you. What if it turned out a friend - or even a family member - was actually gay? Adam, who's your best friend?'

'Blake,' said Adam.

'Yeah, I'd have put money on that,' I muttered to myself just loudly enough, hoping that he had absorbed the remark. 'Okay, what if later today he turned around and told you he was gay?' I asked, expecting him to think twice about his prejudice.

'He's not gay, and I'd tell him I hope he dies of AIDS,'

said Adam, brutally forthright and honest.

'You don't mean that, Adam, do you?' I asked, quickly realising the mentality I was dealing with. And this was a good thing to realise because, in any other setting, I'd have smashed the smug, homophobe's freckled face into last week.

'No,' he said, 'not AIDS. It's just that gays are disgusting and I wouldn't want him near me.' A smattering of heads nodded and agreed. How very disappointing, I thought. 'Do you think I'm disgusting, Adam?' I asked, sincerely.

'I like you, Miss Attwood,' said Felicity, fluttering her eyelashes coquettishly. I could have taken that as a severe piss-take or genuine warm regard. I could even have taken that as a come-on, I remember thinking at the time. But that was certainly best left unsaid. I gave her the benefit of the doubt and discarded her platitude. It didn't matter.

'Thank you, Felicity.' I looked back at Adam.

Adam looked at Felicity. A sort of nineteen-man stand-off was happening in the room. All eyes were on Adam for his response. 'Do you think I'm disgusting, Adam?' I asked once again.

He shifted uncomfortably in the spotlight of his own making. I was hoping above hope he wasn't going to take the easy way out by offering a contrary answer to his real feelings.

'No Miss. You're not disgusting. You're all right, actually. I like you.'

I was genuinely moved by that response. The rest of the class smiled. Perhaps because of the relief of the tension that had been built up.

It was here I learnt the power of The One. This is the student in any class who sets the tone and has most follow his lead. For example, if Jason hates homosexuals, then the majority of the others will, too. If Jason loves Justin Bieber (not that that's likely for a boy to admit) then so do the others. And if Jackass Adam here likes me then the others do. At least, on the surface. For now that's good enough.

'I like you too, Adam,' I said with a smile. Everyone laughed.

I just realised what I had said. You could take that remark a number of ways. I jest. They did smirk, but they knew what I meant. Adam smiled which in turn made me smile.

'In a weird way, guys, what we've just gone through is also lateral thinking, right?' I said.

'How d'you mean, Miss?' asked Felicity. 'Well, you— a lot of you, anyway - believed homosexuality was disgusting. I'm guessing some of you still think it is, and that's okay. Do you know why?' I said. The faces of the kids nodded and agreed with what I was saying.

'Why, Miss?'

'Because I don't give a toss,' I quipped. 'One day you'll learn for yourselves.'

All the children laughed; some at the flippant sentiment, and others because of the word "toss."

There was another person in the room who wasn't laughing for either of those reasons, because she was Belinda Balfour: the deputy head of the school, whom I'd fleetingly met, and was petrified of, in the theatre. She was standing in the half-open door waiting for me to wrap up my class. We locked eyes.

'Ah, er… did you hear what I just said?'

'Indeed I did, Miss.'

The children laughed. A comic moment for them; straight out of the comedy rule book. For me? Possible jail time. Belinda shot me a look as she made her way in properly. 'Sorry Miss Altwild, but it's time for their study skills seminar in the library.'

My first ever class is being cut short!

'Er, okay. Thanks everyone! You guys are awesome!' I was partially lying but needed them to vacate the class having liked me (for all sorts of egotistical reasons.)

'Miss Attwood!' they cheered and laughed, 'you're awesome!'

'Okay everyone, gather your stuff and follow me to the library,' said Belinda. 'Line up outside Miss's classroom, now,' she instructed, turning to me as she walked out. 'Thank you, Miss.'

'Thanks, 'Miss'.' Being called and calling others 'Miss'. That felt weird. The kids smiled at me and said goodbye. Rachel stood up and brushed her hands, looking rather solemn.

'Miss Balfour', said one of the kids to Belinda as they exited the class, 'can we have Mrs Attwood instead of Ms Weir? She's much better.' We didn't get to see the response as the kid peeled off around the corner and into the corridor.

Donna was the last girl to leave, heaving her satchel over her back as she clumsily made for the door. 'Bye Mrs Attwood. Hope we have you next time!' Bye Ms Weir!' she said as she left the room.

Finally, silence. Followed by the emerging squeal of metal, and then -

SCH-TOMPP!! The door slammed shut.

Both Rachel and I juddered at the sound. We slowly turned and stared at each other. I could barely contain my excitement. It was like losing my virginity all over again.

'I TAUGHT MY FIRST CLASS! AGGGHHH!' I exclaimed at the top of my voice, my arms straight by my side, propelling my chest and face up to the sky. The sense of relief was palpable. Rachel closed her eyes and smirked, unimpressed, moving her face back as if my exclamation had just made that famous 'wanker' sign right in her face.

'Yes. Yes, I guess you did,' she said, clearly not as enthralled as I was.

I grabbed Rachel's shoulders and jumped in my shoes. 'I did it! I did it and they liked me! Didn't you see?! My God!' I rambled, 'How? How did I do that?' I asked myself, excitedly. My bottom lip began to quiver. Rachel stepped back, allowing my arms to fall off her shoulders.

'Who knows.' Rachel turned away from me. She drifted slowly to her computer desk and took her seat.

My imagination was racing. My heart pounded. My bottom lip quivered quickly. I knew exactly what this meant.

'Sorry Rachel,' I said, making for the door, 'gimme two seconds.'

'Take your time.'

I left the room. And in the corridor I made a total, sobbing nuisance of myself.

8

You Break the Shooz, You Pay For 'Em

As I pushed my outstretched arms forward and pressed my open palms against the corridor window sill, I could see the class I had just taught walking behind Belinda. They were walking across the playground and heading towards the library. My own reflection was faint in the window as I watched them. It's a weird image; my face with tiny children walking all over it.

There was Adam, the cheeky little runt, walking next to his hella-ugly friend who was sitting next to him during my class. He looked strangely uglier from this distance. Aww, look. Felicity was walking all on her own, with her thumbs hooked under her satchel straps. Donna caught up to Felicity and chatted to her. There was a trio of kids who I didn't recognise at all. Were they in the class? They must have been. I don't remember.

Blake Harwood was being escorted by two police officers across the playground. The kids hadn't noticed as this was happening behind them. Blake's fought them, trying to grab their hands off his shirt collar. I hoped Felicity didn't turn back and see it. Don't turn back, Felicity! Don't turn back!

Felicity turned back and shouted something inaudible at the policemen. It all happened too far away for me to get involved. Judging by their mouths, you could have guessed what was being said. She ran over to Blake and started hitting the officers. Blake shouted at her to go. She's burst into tears.

The officers took Blake away, leaving little Felicity on her knees, sobbing. Belinda came running over to tell her off.

I closed my eyes, turned around and held my head in my hands. I proceeded once again to make a nuisance of myself in the corridor.

Fully drained of water (via my eye ducts), I psyched myself up, ready to walk back into Rachel's classroom. Just as I was about to push Rachel's door open, I looked at laminated glued-on name sign on the door. Earlier this morning it had said "*Ms R. Weir*". It now says "*Ms R. Weirdo*" - the "o" scribbled in red biro. Just underneath it someone else (judging by the handwriting) had been inspired to add "*is a dicksmoking lebsian*" at the end. It's not a typo, incidentally - the last word was mis-spelt.

Is this how students view teachers? I was going to have to make a concerted effort to check every name on every door for the rest of my day here. This was remarkably rude and, actually, quite nasty. I suppose it can happen in any school.

I was now convinced of two things. One, Rachel was clearly not as well regarded by the students as she thought she was. Two, *someone* from period one learnt nothing about irony, judging by their written addendum on her name sign.

I walked into Rachel's classroom and a waft of heat punched my entire body. It was really hot in this room now with the sun beating into it. Then something else jostled for my attention. Rachel tapped away at her computer. Her computer's position meant that she had her back to me, by the white board. I ensured this time that the door didn't slam shut by hooking my finger under the handle and pushing it back softly.

'I just saw that Blake boy getting carried away by the police,' I said.

Rachel didn't turn around. 'Nothing new there. He never learns,' she snapped, carrying on with her work. Her short response wasn't lost on me. Maybe she was genuinely busy.

'This room got warm, didn't it,' I said, making polite inroads to conversation as I walked to her desk.

'Mmm.'

I perched myself on the side of the desk. Next to me were the papers Rachel had been marking when I was teaching. I took the opportunity to thumb through them and have a glance at what marked work actually looked like. Rachel was far too preoccupied with typing on the keyboard.

'How did I do?'

'Mmm,' said Rachel, with a slight pause, 'good.'

Something wasn't right. Rachel was cold-shouldering me. I'm not stupid - Jay had done the exact same move on me twice during the weekend.

'Is everything okay, Raych?'

'Mmm.'

I leaned forward to try to see her face, but Rachel looked down at her keyboard. Her eyes were red. 'Oh my God! Have you been crying? I'm so sorry, I didn't rea—'

'—no, no,' she sniffed, feigning a chuckle. 'I'm just, you know, tired. Think I may be a bit run down.' I smiled and accepted her bullshit answer.

'Ah, yeah, I know that feeling. What you up to?'

'Look,' she snapped. 'I'm a bit busy at the moment. Can you just give me a second, please.'

What nonsense. This woman had been crying. A lot. It must have been to do with me. What had I done to upset this woman?

Actually, you know what? Perhaps it wasn't my fault. Maybe she'd had an argument with her boyfriend, or received a bad text. There was no point ruminating over it. I stood up and took a wander around the teaching-half of her ridiculously narrow class room.

On the wall next to the white board was a big display of things that until now had been invisible to me. Big, colourful bubble writing spelling 'Ms Weir - English & Business' was stuck right at the top of the display. Very eye-catching.

Just underneath that, a similar type of lettering reading 'Tutorial', with Post-It notes underneath; the five weekdays listed one under another. To the right of that, a big picture of something called 'The Marketing Mix', which looked like a four-way diagram. A bunch of cartoon cut-outs of *Sonic the Hedgehog* and *Super Mario*. I'm not sure why they were there, but they added colour to the board.

I read some of the information on an A3 poster called "The Gooder Marking Code". Surely it was meant to say "better"? Then I remembered the name of the school I was at and it all made sense.

"WWW" stood for 'What Was Wonderful', and EBS meant 'Even Better Should…' This must have been what Clive was using earlier for an observation sheet.

'God-damn E-JIT!' exclaimed Rachel, thumping the desk. 'Fucking print for God's sake, you terminally brain-dead bastard!'

Rachel thumped the desk again which, quite by accident, prompted the printer to spring into life and start printing. Rachel swiveled around in her chair to face me. I turned to face her and offered her a smile.

'Wow, you really are user-friendly!' Rachel didn't find this especially funny.

She cleared her throat. 'Okay,' she said, trying not to sniff too much. 'I've arranged a working lunch for you at 1pm with the Communication Skills department.'

'Thanks, that's great.'

'Yeah, and also just a reminder; we've got year eight parents evening at 5:30.'

'Yes, I hadn't forgotten. It's on my schedule,' I said, calmly.

Rachel was definitely upset with me. There's no doubt about it.

'And Joy, don't take this the wrong way but I'd rather you didn't spend lunch with me, if that's okay. I have rather a lot of things to do before period four, but you'll be in good hands with the guys from Comms. Unless of course you get tired of them,' she continued, shrugging her shoulders as if to indicate that that could very well happen. 'Then just feel free to wander around and talk to people you think will help you for your book.'

I stared at Rachel as a blatant teardrop rolled down her face. I was no longer looking at a teacher. I was looking at a student in a uniform trying not to cry because the bigger boys had tormented her. She was very upset, and knew it - and knew I knew it, too, which is probably why she spun around to cover her face and avoid me. She stared at her computer screen and pretended to be busy.

I stepped forward. This needed nipping in the bud now.

'Rachel,' I said softly, walking toward her. 'Thank you for everyth—'

'Aha!' exclaimed a voice from the door behind us. 'You're here, Ms Weir. Oh, that rhymed! Bit of an accident,' said Clive, poking his head in through the door entirely unexpectedly. 'Is now a good time?

Clive was carrying a bunch of papers under his arm and smiling. Rachel quickly rubbed her eyes and took a deep breath. She stood up and turned around, smiling. 'Hi Clive. Yeah, sure, let's get it out of the way.'

'Jolly good,' Clive made for a seat near to her computer desk. 'I know we had arranged for tomorrow break time, but I ran into Belinda and a few kids in the playground. She said that you were free now, so thought I'd take a chance.'

Rachel collected her printout from the printer and folded it in two.

'Suits me,' she said, reaching into her desk drawer.

'Should I stay for this, Rachel?' I asked, hesitantly. Rachel looked into her open desk drawer for something. Clive averted his gaze from Rachel's bent-over bottom to me. 'I'm happy for you to be here. Rachel?'

She looked back into the drawer and took out an envelope. 'Yeah, whatever.'

She aggressively shut the drawer with her knee and sat down opposite Clive at the student's desk. I took a seat at the side of the table between them. I felt like I was adjudicating a thumb war match. Clive put on his spectacles and sifted through his papers.

Rachel slipped the folded printout into the envelope as Clive retrieved the sheet he was looking for - an A4 sheet of paper, with more scribblings in the 'EBS' box than in the 'WWW' one. Way more.

'First of all, thank you for letting me observe you this morning, Rachel,' Clive opened, 'it's always good to observe others as it invariably gives one a clear picture of the class at hand, and also, I find it useful for taking best practise and using it myself.'

Rachel stared him out as she slowly licked the seal of the envelope. This action perturbed Clive, somewhat. Hell, it perturbed me. He didn't know how to react, and so he just kept on talking. 'So I suppose I'll ask you first how you thought—'

'It went shit,' Rachel snapped.

'Oh,' Clive stumbled, not expecting such brutal honesty. 'What makes you think—'

'I didn't prepare.' Rachel interrupted.

'Right. How do you mean?'

'What do you mean "how do I mean"?'

'Well, I mean—'

'Spit it out, chap,' Rachel snapped as she spat the remnants of the envelope glue to the floor. She raised her eyebrows at Clive as if to say "well… ?" It seriously stopped him in his tracks.

'Ahem. Well, I don't think it takes a genius to work out that the class didn't go as you had planned.'

'That's right. I just told you - I didn't plan.'

Puzzled by her uncharacteristically rebellious behaviour, Clive shook his head and adjusted his tie. I was witnessing the wrath of an uniquely put-out Rachel on an unsuspecting man trying to do his job.

'Rachel, what's going on? This is unlike you.'

'No,' Rachel said. 'It's not unlike me at all. What you saw earlier was the real me. The real Rachel.'

'I'm sorry, I'm not following?'

'You're very much like the students at this school in that respect.'

'Rachel?!' Clive exclaimed. 'Has something happened that I'm unaware of? Are you all right?'

'I'm fine, why do you ask?' she snapped, shooting him a look of evil. Clive began to feel the heat and adjusted his collar.

'Yeah, you're right, it is getting hot in here isn't it?' Rachel said, starting to fan her face with her sealed envelope.

'Okay, look, Rachel. I was just trying to get your thoughts on how you think the class went.'

'I already told you it was shit.'

'But what I mean is—'

'Why does every observation always start with "how do you think it went"? What do you care, anyway? Why can't you just say "hey, you fucked up" or "hey, you did okay, but improve this - see ya!"'

'Well, I don't really know—'

'The lesson was shit. The students weren't behaving. I was nursing a hangover. I had just been sick in the car park, didn't get my morning coffee, was in a bad mood and I ran out of time to prepare a class I've taught perfectly well a thousand times before with my eyes closed.'

Rachel tucked her chin under her shirt and slammed the envelope down on the table. She then threw her heels up on the table top.

'Now, Clive. Why don't you tell me how you thought the class went.'

'Well, there was room for improvement, of course.'

Rachel laughed and threw her hands behind her head. She placed her foot on the edge of the desk and pushed her seat back. 'Ahhh, "even better should…". Classic! "EBS" - Egregious Bowel Syndrome!' Rachel laughed, heartily. 'Go on then, what did you think needed improving - apart from absolutely everything?'

Clive scanned his notes.

Rachel banged her heel against the table, startling both Clive and me. 'Stop looking at your fucking notes! Just talk to me man-to-man, tell me.'

'W-well,' Clive said, clearing his throat and becoming anxious, 'clearly the lack of planning had an effect on the rhythm of the class.'

'Uh—huh,' Rachel said as she threw a stick of gum in her mouth.

'You failed to sanction some of the more unruly members of the class.'

'Uh-huh,' Rachel chewed, 'keep it comin'.'

'Also, it was too teacher-centred. Too much TTT, and the kids were getting restless because of it.'

'Sorry, 'TTT'? What's that?'

'Teacher Talk Time,' said Clive. 'The kids weren't involved enough.'

'I agree,' said Rachel, nodding her head.

'So, moving forward, thinking about the future, what-'

'Plan ahead? Get the students to take ownership of their learning?'

'Yes. Right,' said Clive, gathering his papers, indicating he'd had enough. 'I don't know what I did to offend—'

'What grade am I getting?' Rachel barked as she

screwed up her chewing gum wrapper and flicked it over her shoulder. (It landed square in the bin, by the way, although she never saw it.)

Clive didn't deserve this treatment at all. Rachel's behaviour was what we in journalism refer to as a "BNAG" moment; that is to say, "BANG" (out of order).

'Either a three or a four, Rachel,' Clive said, deeply irritated by her behaviour. 'But I think this feedback session has helped me make up my mind. Thank you for your time,' Clive uttered as he picked up his papers and made for the door.

'That's right, get the fuck out of my classroom!' Rachel snapped, angrily.

Clive opened the door and hastily exited the room.

Rachel closed her eyes and took a deep breath. 'Three... two,' Rachel counted as she stood up and straightened her blouse, the distant squeal of metal grew louder, '... one...'

SCH-TOMPP!! The door slammed shut.

'I'm not gonna miss that fucking door, I can tell you,' Rachel muttered to herself, as she stood up and faced me.

I didn't know what on Earth to say. 'Went pretty well I thought?'

Rachel giggled to herself, merrily, and jumped up-and-down on the spot with excitement. 'Man, that felt awesome! Tell me, how did it look. From an objective viewpoint?'

'I, er, well... h-he looked really annoyed after a while.'

'Aww,' Rachel said, beaming with sarcastic vibrancy.

'And I don't think he liked it when you told him to fuck off.'

'I bet the balding insect wasn't expecting that,' Rachel tittered to herself. 'Bet it was a bit of a shock. Probably the first time a teacher behaved like that with him. Fascinating, don't you think?'

I looked at Rachel, puzzled. 'I don't know what to—'

'—I mean, think about it. He's been doing this for

years. Full of grovelling, naive teachers all nodding and agreeing with him,' Rachel said as stood up and slowly drifted toward the window. The sun illuminated her face as she glared at the sky. 'I hope one day when he's regaling his grandkids with his monotonous career stories that he remembers this,' Rachel continued, as she mocked Clive's hulking voice, 'and he says "you know, kids, once there was this teacher who told me to get the fuck out of her classroom." Imagine that, Joy. Imagine yourself immortalised like that in someone's pub stories.'

Rachel gazed at the window in a haze of thoughts. She turned around to face me. 'God, that felt great,' she said. 'If this was a film, I'm guessing the scene would have stopped when the door shut.'

'Well, it is going to be a book.'

'Promise me you'll leave this bit in?'

'Uh, sure. I promise,' I said, just as the classroom door burst open.

It was Gemma on high alert and looking extremely agitated. Rachel and I turned to look at her.

'Ms Weir, I need your help,' Gemma begged. 'It's urgent.'

9

I Called Rambo's Mum and Gave Him a Thousand Lines

Gemma opened the door to her classroom, which was directly opposite Rachel's. We followed her in and were quite astounded by what we saw. A very quiet IT classroom; the majority of the students working obediently well on their computers.

Unlike Rachel's classroom, Gemma's was more typical of what I had expected from a secondary school. For a start, the room was a horseshoe set-up, which means the computer terminals were all lined up around the four walls, with room for the teacher's desk at the front. Neither Rachel or I could see what the issue was until we saw Gemma look over at the corner of her room.

'Walter! Gemma exclaimed. 'For the last time, get out from under there and take your trousers off your head!'

A year nine boy named Walter - in fact, our friend 'the ostrich' from period one - had made himself comfortable under his computer table and had fashioned a makeshift 'Rambo' headscarf with his own pantaloons.

'Ms Weir, Walter refuses to come out,' Gemma said, angrily.

'Is that so, Ms Shortall?' said Rachel.

'That is so, Ms Weir.'

'Walter,' Rachel asked, 'why are you underneath the desk?'

'Dunno.'

'Why are your trousers tied around your head?'

'Dunno.'

'Who tied them around your head?'

'Dunno.'

'Are you going to come out from under the desk?'

'Dunno.'

Gemma shook her head at Rachel. She was on the verge of giving up and letting Rachel take over.

'Walter, listen to me very carefully,' Rachel said calmly as she folded her arms; a common sign that her bullshit-o-meter was starting to crank up. 'If you say "dunno" one more time, I'm going to call home and tell your mum that you're sitting underneath your desk in your pants.'

'Don't care.'

Rachel took out her mobile phone from her pocket and began thumbing the screen. 'Ms Shortall,' Rachel said, as she looked at her phone. 'Can you look up Walter's mum's phone number for me, please.'

'Right away Ms Weir,' said Gemma, as she sat at her computer. Rachel looked at Walter. He looked back at us, concerned.

'You can't do that, Miss!' Walter said.

'Watch me,' Rachel said, poised, ready and eager to enter the number in her phone. 'Sitting in your underpants under your computer desk is also against school rules, genius.'

'That's not allowed in the school. You can't use mobiles,' insisted Walter, hoping it'd at least get Rachel out of the room.

It was patently clear that Walter was saving face in front of the class who, quite understandably, stopped working and had become fascinated by this confrontation. Walter certainly had the attention he so craved, but you could see in his eyes that he was regretting where it was all heading now that Rachel was involved.

'Tell you what, Walter. You keep this ridiculous game going and waste even more of my time, and we'll see who wins, okay?' Rachel said, with a frighteningly vicious smile.

Gemma walked over to Rachel and handed her a Post-It note with Walter's mum's phone number on it. Rachel began typing the number into her phone.

Walter seemed nonplussed. I guess he thought Rachel wasn't going to go through with her threat. He was dead wrong.

'It's ringing,' said Rachel, pressing her phone to her ear. 'Dum-de-dum, c'mon - answer the phone, Mrs Smart.'

By now everyone all eyes were on Rachel. Walter shuffled a bit under the desk.

'Aha. Is that Mrs Smart?' Rachel beamed into the phone. 'This is Ms Weir at Maxwell Gooder's School, it's about Walter,' Rachel said as she eyeballed him. 'No, nothing serious at all. I'm not sure how to say this or even if you'll believe me, but…' Rachel raised her eyebrows at Walter as if to say "last chance, buster".

Taking this to be his last chance, Walter made the right decision and barrel-rolled out from under the desk. He stood up and untied his trousers from his head.

Rachel smiled. 'Walter's doing quite well in English, actually. He made a good contribution to the class this morning during period one.' Walter wafted his trousers, readying himself to climb back into them.

'Incredible', I thought - the way in which Rachel quickly spun the news to Walter's mum in a positive direction, rather than a negative one at a flick of a sentence. I wasn't much afraid for Walter and his dignity with the phone call (after all, his dignity was as far removed from his reputation as his trousers were from his legs). I was afraid for how this ingenious method of getting a defiant child to cooperate may go down with the managers, should they find out about it.

Clearly, though, Rachel didn't care as much. 'I'm quite impressed with his behaviour right now...' she said.

What followed next confirmed - once and for all - that Rachel possessed magic very few others had. She continued on the phone, absorbing his every move.

He pulled apart the waist of his trousers, widening the gap and prepared himself to step into them.

'Yes, his knowledge in the subject is certainly *expanding*.'

Walter then lifted his right leg and inserted it into his trousers.

'He's rarely *put a foot* wrong, in fact.'

And then, his left leg went in. You can imagine the rest.

'In fact he's certainly *landed on his feet* in English. In fact, many kids bend over backwards to to do well, but Walter takes it one step further and *bends over forwards*. He's certainly *reached* as far as he can and really *raised* his 'game'. Actually, he *belted* out his homework quickly and didn't *buckle* under the pressure, at all. So, Mrs Smart, as long as he *tightens* his focus and *straightens out* all the creases, he'll be just fine,' Rachel said.

Walter stood there fully dressed. He had been defeated. The rest of the class felt like laughing and whooping, but knew Rachel was on the phone and didn't want to disturb her. Rachel bit down on her tongue to stop herself from laughing.

'Well, teachers rarely get an opportunity to call with good news. My pleasure. Many thanks, Mrs Smart. Goodbye.' Rachel killed the call with her thumb and put her phone in her pocket.

Everyone cheered and clapped. Rachel took a bow, as the jeering reached its frenzied climax.

Walter's embarrassment was both well-earned and, well, embarrassing. Rachel smirked at Walter and wiggled her index finger at him as the laughter continued.

'Okay, dickhead. My room. Now.'

Rachel held her classroom door open for Walter. He sauntered in, prepared for war. I followed into the classroom with Rachel close behind me.

Walter spun around to Rachel, angrily. 'I'm going to report you to Mr Nutella.'

'Oh yeah? And what exactly are you going to tell Mr Martelle?'

'Fucking Weirdo.'

'You wish.'

'I'll tell him what happened - that you embarrassed me in front of the class and that you called my mum and called me a dickhead.'

'Interesting,' Rachel retorted. 'Are you going to tell him how it all started, as well?' That stopped him in his tracks.

'Besides, I never called your mum.'

'Yes you did! I saw you!'

'Nah, I faked it. The phone never rang.'

'Bullshit. Show me the note.'

A clever bit of detective work from Walter, there. The note would reveal that she had the number.

'Here you go,' Rachel offered him the note. He took it and scanned it. Having absorbed the information, he screwed the note up and viciously threw it to the floor. It landed by my foot.

'Fuck's sake!' Walter screamed, thumping the wall with his fist.

'You don't make life easy for yourself, do you?' Rachel asked. 'Why do you keep acting the wanker whenever you're in Miss Shortall's class, anyway? Every day last week, wasn't it?'

''Cuz it's boring.'

'Walter, one day you'll learn, maybe when you're older, that when you're bored in a job or feel like something isn't worth doing, you just shut up and say nothing. Get through the day as best you can. You know?'

'I never understand what Shortarse tells us to do. She just says "go on the computers and get on with coursework." I dunno what I'm doing.'

'Okay,' Rachel continued, trying to fix the situation. 'So

if it happens again, instead of acting the dick what will you do?'

'Knock her out?'

'Walter, that's a violent threat. I'll have to report you for that,' Rachel explained, as she looked at me. 'I have Miss here as a witness.' This information took a few seconds for Walter's brain to fully process.

I picked the sticky note up from the floor and read the contents. 'Murder him for me, sweetie. Thanx much, G x.'

I tittered quietly to myself and handed the sticky note to Rachel. She folded it in four and pocketed it. 'Now,' Rachel said. 'Try again.'

Walter sighed, exasperatedly. 'Ugh. Ask for help, or find the answer for myself?' he said, as if reciting a mantra he'd heard from various teachers a thousand times before.

'Good. Now, sit here in the quiet corner.'

Rachel turned to me as Walter he reluctantly took his seat. 'Miss, can you fetch me some lined paper and a pen, please.' I went to the computer desk and picked up some lined paper and a pen from a pot.

I returned and sat a pen and sheet of lined paper down in front of Walter. He picked up the pen, angrily.

'Now,' Rachel ordered, 'write out "I won't undress in front of my class and hide underneath a table" a thousand times. Or until till the bell for lunch goes, whichever is the sooner'.

'Whaaat!?' Walter uttered to himself.

Rachel smiled and winked at me behind Walter's back. He thumped the pen on the table. I didn't know how to respond. My knowing smirk must have come out like a silent, wet mouthfart to him.

'Just shut up and do it.'

Moments later and Walter was in the thick of his line writing.

My friends and I joked about how easy kids had it in school these days, particularly with the invention of computers. We often chuckled over the fact that, if we were given lines today, we'd just jump on a computer and copy and paste them in seconds flat.

Watching Walter fill out his lines on traditional lined paper was proof that sometimes our benevolence toward technology doesn't always get us out of tight spots. I'll give Walter this, though - he can write really fast. Clearly the result of a lot of hours of practice.

Walter sort of reminded me of myself when I was at school. Though less obtuse, I was a world-class liar. A straight-A student. My high school years taught me how to conceal things I didn't want revealed and, most importantly, how *not* to learn subjects. I mastered the art of appearing to be attentive in class, when what I was actually doing was doodling illustrations of unicorns in the back of my textbook.

I was a master of apathy, allergic to knowledge; I escaped five entire years of content in a variety of subjects and grew my ignorance to extraordinarily impressive heights.

My reward was the absence of any GCSEs that could have got me into college. Obtaining a degree was out of the question. I had earned this reward outright. I then deeply regretted it when I entered the job market aged sixteen, forever consigned to a lifetime earning the minimum wage.

I looked at Rachel's marked papers. She pulled out an example which was full of red ink.

'The school has a code to make marking easier,' she explained. 'So if a kid spells something wrong, we write 'sp' in red next to it. If it's a grammar error, then 'gr' and so on.'

'How long does it take to mark a class's work, usually?'

'Far too long. This pile, twenty-three students, maybe three minutes each. You do the mathematics.'

I tried. Three times twenty-three. Think, Joy. Ahh! Think quicker. You're looking like an idiot in front of

Rachel, for God's sake!

'I'll save you the bother, it's sixty-nine.'

'Yeah I was just about to say,' I lied, hoping she wouldn't cotton on.

Rachel chuckled to herself. 'Anyway, this is just one class. An hour of my life marking? Up to twenty classes per week?' Rachel scanned her brain as she rattled on. 'Christ, I've never said this out loud before, but that's twenty-three hours of bastard marking per week. Fuck me.'

'That's impossible!' I said.

'No kidding. But there's a very simple solution.'

'Is there?'

'Yes.'

'What?'

'Don't mark it,' Rachel giggled evilly as she pulled out some examples. 'Want to see?'

10

Dr Barnum: Or How I Learned to Stop Worrying and Not Mark Work

Okay, this was a new one. I could believe the endless smoke breaks; the fly-by-your knickers approach to teaching; the soft blackmailing of students; the cocaine being snorted out of desk drawers in full view of students and the potential abuse of girls in their own toilets. But this? Not marking? I was looking forward to Rachel trying to convince me that this would work.

'It's simple,' Rachel began. 'Have you ever heard of *Barnum statements*?'

'No?'

'Right. To cut a long story short, psychics use it when they're telling fortunes. Sometimes it's called cold reading but, essentially, they are statements that make broad, sweeping generalisations.' Rachel said, as if giving a seminar. She has clearly rehearsed this speech in her mind many times over.

'What's that got to do with marking work?'

'Well, okay. I'm going to read your mind. Ready?'

'Sure?'

Rachel closed her eyes and waved her index finger a few inches from my nose. She pressed her palm against her forehead with her other hand.

'Ooooh. Uh-huh. Okay, I'm getting the letter 'B' and

'T' in your mind,' Rachel said, opening her eyes. I twitch, uncomfortably, still confused. 'Something significant starting with the letter 'B',' Rachel said, acting the psychic as her right forefinger hovered inches from my eyes.

'Yes, my Dad's name was Brian!'

'That's right, Brian,' Rachel continued. 'And he's passed over to the other side, hasn't he?' I squirmed inside. It was spooky.

'Yes,' I said. 'He died two years ago.'

'On or near your wedding, am I right?'

'Piss off! How did you know that!?'

'Am I right?' Rachel asked, still hovering her finger around my face. 'Y-yes,' I stuttered, feeling pensive. 'You're right.'

Rachel laughed, closed her fist and knocked me on the shoulder. 'Ha. A sucker born every minute.'

'How did you know that about my Dad, and that he passed away two years ago? Are you a real psychic?'

Rachel huffed and smiled. 'Oh, shut up. You told me everything.'

'I did not! And you know I didn't.'

'Are you sure?' Rachel snapped, happy with herself.

Had I told her everything? Was I dreaming?

'Look, I said the letters 'B' and 'T'. Statistically, one if not both of those letters was bound to have meaning for you, right? Somewhere?' Rachel said, getting impatient with my own naivety.

'Well, sure, I guess.'

'So, obviously there's a connection somewhere. It could have been a pet name, or the name of your first doll—'

'Yes, but how did you know my Dad's name was Brian?'

'You told me! You said "Yes! Yes! His name was Brian!" like a daft canary. I asked if he had died, and you said "yes" which was a total fluke. It's called fishing. If you had said "no", I'd have flipped on a dime and said "yes, of course, he's still alive which is why I can't see him",'

Rachel said, almost sincerely angry that I had been so gullible. 'Don't you ever give information away like that again!'

I searched my cranial browsing history but couldn't recollect doing anything she had accused me of. I gave her the benefit of the doubt. I was deeply confused, but it seemed to have made sense. However, there's one detail she would never be able to explain.

'Ah. But how did you know he died just after Jay and I got married? I never revealed that. I've never revealed that to anyone.'

'Correct, you never revealed that. But that was easy.'

'Was it?'

'Yeah, you said he died two years ago. Gay marriage was legalised about two years ago. I'm guessing you guys got married right away. You seem the impatient type. It was a punt worth taking, and it paid off.'

She was right. She'd gleaned I was impatient. Jay and I did want to get married as soon as it had been legalised. It all makes sense now. I feel so stupid. Rachel has shown a creepy, narcissistic side to herself.

'Why did you do that to me?'

'To make a point about something else. Look,' Rachel said, smugly. She showed me three separate pieces of the same work, all marked in red. 'Notice anything similar about these three 'randomly-selected' pieces of work?'

I scanned the documents and found her red comments difficult to read. But there was a pattern to them. The same number of words in the margins. I leaned in for a closer look and read them out loud.

"This is a good point, but how could you develop this idea?" I read.

'Yep,' Rachel continued. 'Noticed anything similar between these?'

I looked and eventually saw what she was talking about. I raised my eyebrows. 'They all say the same thing.'

'Yes,' Rachel confirmed. 'That's right, they do.'

'So what's so unusual about that?' I asked. I was a bit lost.

'Much like the cold reading I gave you, I do the same thing with comments like this. With marking work.' Rachel revealed.

As I sifted through the seemingly endless piles of papers, it slowly dawned on me what Rachel had been doing. She's repeating vague comments that invited the student to produce more work. It looked as if it was thoroughly marked.

'Rachel, are you saying that you haven't read a single one of these papers!?' I asked, in a way that Walter couldn't overhear.

'Nope. Not a single one.'

'But some of them have even responded in green with answers!'

'Yep,' Rachel giggled. 'Works every time.'

'So you just mark without reading what they write?'

'That's a good point, Joy,' Rachel said. 'But tell me, how could you develop that idea?' I was knocked for seven, let alone six.

'Because you can't be bothered to read it?' I asked.

'That's a good point, Joy. Develop that idea?'

'Because... I dunno, you don't have time?'

'Good. Keep going. Develop the idea.'

The penny dropped. It was no different to the old trick we used to irritate teachers with when I was at school; you kept asking 'why?' all the time, trying to rattle their cage. Nevertheless, this was quite a revelation and hard to digest.

'But,' I whispered, wide-eyed, 'that's insane! Aren't you afraid of getting caught?' I asked, genuinely quite concerned.

'Oh please, yes. I am dying for the day I get caught. It means someone would be paying attention to me and my work!' Rachel said. Is that true, I wondered? Does no-one ever spot-check or examine the quality of the marking?

'Do you think anyone on this planet has enough time

to actually forensically scan each document, let alone compare notes?' Rachel barked, satisfied with her own answer.

'But what about the moral implications? And the ethical considerations?'

Rachel shot me a look, dead-set. 'Are you out of your tiny little mind?'

I blinked my eyes rapidly; the good nature inside me upturned, and pulled inside-out. I believed this was a legitimate question which needed answering.

'Joy, this job vacuums my time, thoughts and marriage. I get paid peanuts. You average out all the hours I work here and at home marking and planning and it equates to less than minimum wage. Don't you dare talk to me about morality or ethics when it comes to teaching. It's the single-most corrupt profession in the country. Well, next to banking and prostitution, anyway.'

Okay, now the truth was out, I guess. 'I have a bank of 'feedback loops', as I call them,' Rachel said. 'All committed to memory. It's called *TRAGIC VIEW* which, in some ways, is pretty poetic as it perfectly summarises my stance on the profession.'

'Tragic View?' I asked.

'Yeah,' Rachel said. 'It's possibly the first acronym in education that is of actual, physical use to a teacher. It takes about ten minutes to memorise; but if that's the difference between six hours of genuine marking, or half an hour of 'faux' bullshit that does the job just as well, then I consider it ten minutes well spent.'

Anecdotally, TRAGIC VIEW - much like its name - is an acronym for the most deceptive short-cut in teaching I've ever encountered. Rachel insisted that it doesn't exist in any textbook and (at time of writing) hasn't even found its way onto the internet - it's that secretive, apparently.

I've listed the ten 'feedback loops' that connect TRAGIC VIEW below, for reference. Rachel said that each and every one can be used when marking work, no matter where in the sentence you make the comment.**

This could be worded slightly better, (but it'll do/please address)
Really not sure I agree. Could you clarify/counter argue?
An excellent idea, I wish I'd thought of that!
Good!* *(Use sparingly)*
Interesting *(keep an eye on this, no more than two per work)*
Can you expand on this idea?
Very good! *(Don't use this too often)*
I know you know this, but can you reveal why you think this?
Excellent!* *(See above)*
What would happen if this weren't the case?

*If you get really stuck for variation, accompany with a 'smiley face'.

** Neither I nor anyone connected to this book can accept responsibility if you choose to enact this method of marking and get caught. Discretion is advised.

Rachel slid a marked piece of work under my nose. 'Look at this. This is the kind of English we have to deal with on a daily basis.'

I read the paper as best I could. Even by my poor literary standards, I could tell this student wasn't able to write properly at all. Here's an extract of what I saw, minus the corrections.

When u ran a bussiness u ned to come up wiv a good ideas or. It wil the conpany u set up will go busted and it wont be abel to make more profit and it will make them loose there job.

Where to start when marking a piece of work like this? This was damn-near incomprehensible. 'That's true. Using 'feedback loops' practically impossible. It's probably the only work that ever gets genuinely read, which makes it doubly annoying.'

'What year is this student in?

'Year eleven,' Rachel said. 'Carly's about to take her GCSEs at the end of the month. Beginning next week, actually.'

'She's definitely dyslexic,' I said.

'Yes,' Rachel agreed. 'Guess what grade I gave it.'

'I dunno. An F?'

Rachel snorted like I was an idiot. 'What, and murder her self-esteem and confidence right before her GCSEs? With my results on the line? Nawww,' Rachel laughed as if I'd farted, 'I gave it an "A".'

'An "A"!? You're joking, surely?'

'Yes, an "A". And no, I'm not joking,' Rachel explained. 'Carly's answer is from a GCSE Business practice question. The trick here is that you're marking the content, and not the English. Look, you and I know she'll get an F in the exam. Carly probably knows it, too. But if I tell her it's piss-weak, then she will get an F.'

Rachel showed me the A with a green circle around it.

'What if I slip her a nudge of encouragement? The planets may just align and by some fluke she could get a higher grade. I'll take a *could* over a *won't*, every time. I'm not going to jeopardise my reputation and her thin chances of success. So, an A for content and ignore the English.'

My hopes and dreams for teachers being the arbiters of honesty and goodness all but vanished into thin air at this point. The plot was just getting more and more ridiculous, I thought. 'So doesn't she get any help, like a special tutor?' I enquired.

'Nope. Carly is PP, so her folks are unlikely to be able to afford extra tuition. She's meant to be have LSA in class, but I've never seen one,' Rachel explained. I was baffled by these initials.

'What are all those initials?'

'Ugh, they're the bane of my life, that's what they are. PP is 'Pupil Premium'. Back in our day it would have been called 'free school dinners', which means they're from a low income family.'

'But why should that matter?' I asked.

'I personally don't think it does, but in the eyes of our wonderful Eton-bred government, I guess they see the poorer amongst us as low-achievers; destined for the dole queue. For example, if mum is a part-time check-out girl, and dad is unemployed, then that's probably what the kid's future as an adult is going to be.'

I squirmed hearing the honesty of the explanation. 'So, pupil premium kids are slapped with the third class citizen brush before they've even walked in the door?' I asked.

Rachel looked over at Walter and saw that he had stopped writing.

'Oi! Smart-arse! Why aren't you writing?' Rachel barked. Walter turned around and screwed up his face.

'My wrist hurts, Miss. I'm taking a break.' Rachel sniggered to herself. She was thinking of exactly the same punchline as me.

'Okay, you've had a break, now keep on writing'.

It was 1:27pm. The prospect of a free lunch (there is such a thing for guests at Maxwell Gooder's!) was making me giddy; both with anticipation, and also as an unfortunate symptom of type 2 diabetes.

As Rachel was clearing the papers away, a book fell to the floor. She quickly bent over to pick up and surreptitiously slipped it under her papers. She had the face of a little girl caught with her hand in the candy jar. I couldn't resist knowing why she had been pathetically secretive about covering her tracks.

'What's that book?' I asked. 'That's not a curriculum book.'

'Well if you must know it's a book on writing.'

That made sense to me. If you're an English teacher, surely you'd be staying match-fit and keeping up with the changes in your subject. Rachel slid the book in front of me. The cover said everything I needed to know.

"Self-Publish Your Fiction Today!"

I pondered this for a while and let it sink in. Why is Rachel reading this book? This wasn't something a teacher can use to teach children. But, alas, Rachel's look said it all. She wasn't brushing up on English. I think her face is told me something far more drastic.

'Rachel,' I snapped, urgently. 'I need to ask you one last question—'

And then - as if some omnipotent, crazy and sadistic author were writing our story - the bell for lunch rang and cockblocked my groove.

'Okay,' Rachel roared at Walter, causing him to jump. 'Get outta here.' Walter stood up and bolted towards the door. He yanked the door open and ran back to his class. I stood up and stretched my arms out. It felt good.

'Time for lunch!' Rachel said, smiling at me. 'The question will have to wait. See you period five!'

SCH-TOMPP!! The door slammed shut.

11

No Rice for the Wicked

'Is this all there is? Chips?' I asked, surprised. The pudgy dinner lady serving food from behind the school canteen counter didn't even look at me.

'Yeah,' she blurted out, barely containing her contempt for those not wearing the same overalls as her.

'Do you have any rice?'

'We did. But we've run out. Chips is all we got.'

'But lunch has only just started. When did you run out?'

'Week last Thursday.'

Unimpressed, I shuffled along the counter with my decidedly unhealthy-looking "Swedish-style meatballs in button mushroom cream", wondering what on earth the kids were going to be eating. Indeed, this question was answered as I counted more children with boxes of chips than with any other culinary item.

The canteen itself was a bit like the school's theatre; only smaller, and produced less of an echo on account of the deafening tirade of screaming, chatting and occasional singing on behalf of its frequenters.

I could have sworn there was a sign above the entrance saying "Bet you wish you'd brought a packed lunch, eh?" but to be honest the hunger was starting to get to me.

'We had a whole week of tutorials based on healthy eating,' came a voice from behind me to anyone who was listening. 'Told them how they needed their five a day. Eat fresh vegetables and drink water instead of fizzy drinks. And what does the canteen serve? Chips.' The man tutted and shook his head, quickly reducing his neighbouring colleagues to knowing smirks.

The shaking head belonged to Head of Communication Skills, Jeremy Sassoon. We took our seats at a folded-out plastic table and seat arrangement, opposite one another. I gazed at my meatballs, prodding one around with my plastic fork. Predictably, one of the prongs snapped and flew off over my shoulder. If the food was anything as good as the plastic cutlery, I should have booked myself a room at the hospital a month ago.

'So Jeremy,' I asked, trying not to look at my sweating meatball lunch, 'where does the Communication Skills department fit within the overall curriculum?'

Jeremy said something, but I was damned if I could make it out seeing as he was attempting to talk with his mouth full. Just then we were joined by two of his own department's teachers. They also happened to be husband and wife; Norman and Kitty Bakewell. Both seemed extremely tired.

Kitty took a seat beside me and Norman sat next to Jeremy. As they greeted one another, it was clear that all three of them had known each other a while, and bore the bruises of pedagogical battlement for far longer than any other teacher I'd met so far today.

'I had to put Lawrence Diehl in school detention,' Norman said to Jeremy, as he poured himself a cup of water. 'You want a fill?'

'Yeah, please,' Jeremy said. 'Why'd you give him a det?'

'He called Jacob a *nignoramous*.'

'Which one?'

'Jacob Adewala, who do you think!?'

'Oh right. Yes, of course.'

'He's hardly gonna called Jacob Goldman a nignoramous, is he?' Norman spat, as Kitty leaned over to

146

face him.

'Norm, can you stop saying that word, please.'

Norman cleared his throat and hushed. 'Sorry'. He finished pouring Jeremy's water and put the jug back onto the table.

When I think back to my own school days, teachers were just robots to us kids. They never ate, never used the toilet (because they never ate) and never left the school. In fact, my friends and I used to joke that they all walked into the staff room at 3:30pm each day and plugged themselves into a nearby wall socket and powered down. Now that I'm older I can see the humanity behind the perpetual look of stress.

'So, Joy,' Kitty said. 'How did you find the school?'

'I asked a couple of students where—'

'—no,' she interrupted. 'I mean, how are you liking it?'

'Oh. Yes, well,' I scrambled for an answer, 'it's enlightening.'

Kitty seemed satisfied with my terse response. We all returned to our food in a thinly veiled attempt to avoid talking to one another. I was keen to discover more about the team, but decided to satiate my hunger before trying anything too probing.

'Oh!' Kitty exclaimed. 'Did you hear, Ms Harwood in FML swore at a kid in French class?

'Ms Harwood?' I asked, realising that this surname is cropping up rather a lot. 'Sounds familiar.'

'Yeah,' Kitty said. 'French teacher. She has three kids here at the school.'

'What's FML?'

'Foreign Modern Languages,' said Kitty, 'and yes, the kids laugh at it. The management haven't cottoned-on yet, I don't think.'

'Nope,' Norman added. 'Much funnier to not say anything!'

'What did she say?' Jeremy asked, as he smiled at me.

'Who are you asking?' Norman said.

'I didn't say anything,' Kitty responded.

'No,' Jeremy said, shoving a spoonful of mash into his mouth. 'Mrs Harwood. What did she say?'

'Oh. "Shut your fucking face you little faggot", apparently.'

'Really!' Jeremy exclaimed with his mouthful. 'In French?'

'Yes.'

'So, what's that in French?' Norman enquired.

'What's what in French?'

'"Shut your fucking face you little faggot"?' Norman asked.

'Don't call me a faggot.' Jeremy said, as he gouged out some meat remnants from between his two front teeth with his index finger.

'No, stupid,' Norman said. '"What's "shut your fucking face you little faggot" in French?'

'It begins with "close" -- ferme, doesn't it?' Jeremy asked. 'It's... Ferme ta putain... de gueule, something...?'

'No!' Kitty said. 'She said it in French, in English!'

'When did Ms Harwood start teaching English?' Norman asked, totally confused.

'She doesn't,' Kitty said, getting impatient. 'She said it in French in English.'

'She said it in two different languages?'

'No!'

I was starting to miss Rachel. Trying to make sense of my bizarre encounter with the Communication Skills Department, I found myself exiting the canteen into the gloriously warm and humid playground. The sun was beating down on me in much the same way that a sixth former was doing to a year ten boy at the far end of the playground.

A chorus of 'Boooooooos!' echoed across the cement rectangle as a batch of random kids went running over to see the fight close up. Across the other end of the playground, there was a teacher who was on lunchtime duty. He was wearing a high viz jacket with his hands in his pockets. He stared widely at his shoes as he paced around. The resulting chanting and encouragement caught the teacher's attention, so he ran over to try to break it up.

My stomach still grumbling, and the heat getting to me, I felt it was a good idea to head back to reasonably familiar territory. I headed toward the Food Technology Department (which in turn would lead me near to Rachel's classroom). A young girl came walking the other way. I recognised her face. It was Felicity from period three with two girls walking alongside her whom I didn't recognise.

'Hey Miss!' Felicity said as we walked past each other.

'Hey Felicity!' I said with a smile. As she and her friends continued walking away from me, I heard Felicity say something along the lines of "she's the best teacher."

I didn't turn around. I'm not even sure as I write this that that was what she said. But it felt like she said it and that's all that matters.

I reached the middle playground. The two adjacent buildings of classrooms either side were looming over me, seemingly scanning my every move. Sure enough, there were CCTV cameras at each end of both buildings. A few boys were perched at the side of the building, leaning against the wall. One of them wolf whistled at me as I walked by them. 'Afternoon, Miss! Nice jeans!' said one of them, chuckling to his peers. I ignored it, and walked on.

In front of me was the reception area. To my left, I think, the maths department. I realised something that was bound to happen sooner or later - I was lost. So, I did what anyone would do and continued forward.

I pushed through the double swing doors, and found myself at reception. A tiny little girl in a Maxwell Gooder uniform was sitting on the visitor couch and looked at me apologetically. She smiled and fluttered her eyes, trying to win my affection. She was presumably hoping I wouldn't be yet another adult who'd yell at her today.

I looked right, and up. Aha! There was that damn Picasso painting thing again! What was that meant to be? It looked like a car scrap yard, with party poppers strewn from the middle; reds, blues and whites. A streak of what looks like spit spattered up from the middle into an elongated V-shaped firework explosion.

'Oh, Joy!' exclaimed a familiar voice from behind me. 'What are you doing here?'

I turned around. It was Rachel. She must have been several footsteps behind me.

'Rachel! What are you doing here!' She took a defensive stance and bowed her head like the little girl on the couch had done a moment or so ago. Rachel, just in that one move, looked like a student and not a teacher.

I noticed Rachel had an envelope in her right hand. She quickly tucked it behind her back and glanced over at the year seven girl, expertly directing attention away from her hand. But, still, I had noticed her doing it. I think she knew that I'd seen everything.

'Sophie.'

'Hello, Miss,' Sophie squeaked, in the most butter-melting way.

'Your skirt is riding a bit high, isn't it?' Rachel asked. 'Probably best to turn it down a bit. What do you think?'

I get the impression that Rachel turned her attention to deliberately avoid me. I could have been wrong, though. Perhaps the general paranoia teachers carried with them was starting to rub off on me. I had taught a class, after all. So now, technically, I was a legitimate teacher. Sort of.

'Yes, Miss,' Sophie said. She stood up and pulled the hem of her skirt down past her knees. 'Sorry, Miss.'

'That's better, Sophie.' Rachel said, as she peered over toward reception. I stepped with her. 'Rachel, I just wanted to apolog—'

'Gail?' Rachel said, interrupting me.

Gail looked up from behind the reception. 'Yes, hello.'

'Is Mr Martelle available? I need to see him, it's quite urgent.'

'I'll just call him and find out, hold on,' Gail said, picking up her phone.

'You reek of cigarettes, Raych. Are you okay?' I asked, genuinely concerned about her welfare. She seemed stressed and frazzled. Her attitude had changed since period three. It was also patently clear where Rachel had been spending the first half of the lunch break. Very definitely in her "main office".

'Yeah sure, why wouldn't I be?' Rachel snapped.

'Look, I just want to apolog—' I began, as we turned to watch Gail answer the phone.

'Hello, Mr Martelle. It's Gail. I wondered if—'

She paused to listen to the voice on the other end of the phone.

'It's me, Gail. On reception. Yes, I wondered if you could—'

She paused again. 'Gail. At Maxwell Gooder's school reception? Yes. I wondered if you were free at the minute, as I have someone at reception who's wanting a quick word. I'm not sure, let me ask.'

Gail held her left hand over the mouthpiece. 'What's it about?' she asked Rachel.

'Tell him it's urgent, but that it shouldn't take very long.'

'She says it's not very urgent, but it might take a while.' Gail said, erroneously. Rachel shot me a look that simply said "kill me now."

'Yes, it might be in reference to the Harwood incident, I don't know. Okay. Okay, I will. Bye.' Gail hung up the receiver, and returned to her work. Rachel turned to me, vacantly, and then back to Gail.

'Well?' Rachel snapped, violently. 'What'd he say?'

'Oh. Yes, you can go in.'

Rachel turned to me once again, and tried for a smile.

Rachel turned to me once again, and tried for a smile. 'Well, Joy. Here it is. Moment of truth.' She revealed the envelope from behind her back. 'I've shown you how to handle meetings, prepare for a class, teach a class, deal with unruly behaviour, reward good behaviour and deal with mischievous students,' Rachel said, proudly. 'There's just one thing left to show you.'

'And what's that?' I asked.

Knock Knock.

'Come in,' said the voice behind the head teacher's door. Rachel pushed the door open, and we walked into the head teacher's office.

'Ah, do come in,' Mr Martelle said as he stood up and offered her a seat at his conference table (I say "conference table" - it was more like one of those cheap FjucKopf & Die glass dinner table nightmares from IKEA).

Rachel took a seat opposite Mr Martelle as he launched into an apology. 'I am most sorry. I'm afraid we're in a bit of a tizzy at the moment. One of our year eleven boys was arrested today, and we're trying to hunt down the owner of a Gold Ford Fiesta that was acting suspiciously earlier this morning. So it's all go!'

'Actually, I think—' I said, before being interrupted.

'Forgive me,' Mr Martelle said to Rachel, 'but could you remind me of your child's name again, Mrs—?'

'—Weir. Ms Weir,' Rachel said. 'I don't have any children.'

'Oh, duh. Silly me!' Mr Martelle said, correcting himself. 'Of course. Yes, I'm so sorry.'

'That's quite all right.'

'So, you're here for the position of Teacher of English and Business.'

'I *am* the fucking Teacher of English and Business!' Rachel exclaimed, with a glaze of anger swimming through her eyes. She slammed the envelope down on the table.

'That is, until the end of term, anyway. Here's my resignation.'

She pushed the envelope toward Mr Martelle. Puzzled, he took the envelope and opened it.

Rachel looked at me. I looked back at her. 'What are you doing?' I mouthed, stunned.

She turned to face Mr Martelle as he read the contents. As he began reading, Rachel just continually stared at him, barely able to contain her unremitting anger. My heart began to flutter. Was she resigning because of me? Surely not.

'Uh-huh. Mmm,' Mr Martelle muttered as he read. 'Ah, ha. Yes, good point. Mmm. Okay, very good.' Mr Martelle put the letter down.

'So, my last day of term will be July 22nd,' Rachel said. 'Of course I'm willing to take part in any handover exercise you'd need me to do.'

'That's very kind of you. Tell me Cheryl, is—'

'Rachel.'

'Yes, yes, of course,' Mr Martelle corrected himself. 'Rachel. Is your leaving anything to do with the school?'

'Not especially,' Rachel offered, calming down. 'It's just the job. I've had enough. In fact I think it's had enough of me.'

Mr Martelle nodded his head slowly, trying to feign sympathy with a staff member he clearly didn't know and whom was about to become someone he'd continue to not know for the foreseeable future. What's more, she'll have to be replaced sometime very soon.

'Well thanks for stopping by. I wish you well for the future. I'll have Belinda email you a leaver's exit form as soon as we get the damned E-JIT working again.' Mr Martelle said, extending his hand for her to shake. She took his hand and shook it. Firmly.

'Thank you, Mr Martelle.'

'Please, call me Craig,' Mr Martelle said. 'I'd like to say on behalf of the school and the students, that we will miss you and appreciate all the hard work you've done for us, Cheryl.'

'Thanks.' Rachel said, deciding it better to just let it go. She suddenly went quiet and darted out of the room.

Well, this was awkward. Mr Martelle and I alone together in his office having just witnessed Rachel hand in her notice. I couldn't bear the silence. I don't think he could, either.

'Sorry.' apologised Mr Martelle, to no-one in particular.

I had to break the silence somehow and said the only thing that popped into my head.

'Actually, while I'm here, Mr Martelle, do you have time for a quick interview?'

He thought about it for a few seconds. 'Yes. Yes, okay. Why not,' he said, comfortable with his decision. 'Remind me, which agency are you from?'

'I'm not from any agency' I explained. 'I'm from Chrome Valley Books.'

'Right, right. Yes, of course,' Mr Martelle said, with a smile that indicated politeness but utter incredulity.

'Yes. *In Their Shoes.*'

'What is?'

'I'm sorry?

'What's in their shoes?

'No,' I said, trying to veer him back on track, 'remember, the documentary about teaching? We spoke by email?'

'Oh!' said Mr Martelle, suddenly realising who I was. 'Yes of course, please do take a seat.'

I sat down opposite him as he cleared his papers - and Rachel's resignation - to one side. He pressed his palms together, readying himself. 'I say, it's most unusual all this. But I do enjoy new challenges.'

'Yes.' I placed my voice recorder on the table. 'You don't mind me doing this, do you?'

'Not at all.'

I pressed the record button and began the interview.

Mr Martelle shifted around in his seat. 'I see. Jolly good. Most unusual for candidates to record their own interviews. Then again, I was privately educated.'

'Oh, actually it's not that unusual at all,' I explained. 'It's more for clarity, I suppose. I don't want to misquote or misrepresent you in any way.'

'Splendid. So, first things first I suppose. Do you have any experience with the English and Business curricular?' Mr Martelle asked, clearly struggling with the concept of ends of sticks.

I spent the next fifteen minutes explaining my intentions to little effect and subsequently decided to make my excuses and leave, for both our sakes.

12

Attack Their Character

It was 2:45pm - exactly half way through the final period of the day. Maxwell Gooder's school day concludes at 3:20pm.

As I made my way toward Rachel's classroom, I felt a bit confused about a number of things. Chief among them was just how this school was able to manage to remain fully functioning, considering the dynamic of the staff that inhabited the classrooms and corridors of the building. For every right-minded and pragmatic individual I'd encountered there was someone equally as listless or downright confused as I was. Then again, could this be true of every workplace? Whether it be a school or common-or-garden office?

I made my way up the purple stairwell and toward the English corridor. It was post-lunch and the empty, ketchup-smeared chip boxes strewn across the floor greeted me as I ascended the stairs.

Careful to avoid slipping on a discarded banana skin (yes, even here!), I gripped the stair rail to protect my balance. As my hand squeezed it, I felt a slimy, wet substance French kiss the skin of my palm. Upon closer inspection it appeared to be some sort of gelatinous yellow stuff. It was either mustard or vomit and, as the canteen didn't serve hot dogs, I decided that it must have been the latter. My next course of action hastily altered, I decided to head to the nearest visitor toilet.

I reached the English corridor and made my way past Rachel's classroom. Adjacent to that, Gemma's classroom was empty. The door was propped open with a fire extinguisher. I peered inside, careful not to touch anything with my contaminated left hand. Gemma was sitting at her computer desk, her elbows propping up her head in her hands.

'Uh, hello?' I said. 'Gemma, isn't it?'

Gemma looked up, red-eyed. She'd clearly been crying during her free period. She quickly snorted and smiled. 'Oh, hi, Joy. You okay?' She noticed my out-turned left palm.

'Jeez, what happened to your hand?' she asked, wiping her eyes with her sleeve.

"Yes. I, uh, think I touched something on the stair rail. Do you know where the nearest toilet is?'

'Yes, it's two doors down, just before the double doors.'

I continued down the corridor, following her instructions and passed by another classroom. The door was shut, but you could hear the "Shut up!"'s and "Calm down!"'s thundering through the walls.

Further down the corridor in another classroom, an extremely well-behaved set of pupils were undertaking a paper-based test. The teacher paced around studiously with her arms folded ensuring that they didn't speak or cheat. She shot me a look. I turned the other way pretending not to have seen anything.

Then, I arrived at the "staff and visitor only" toilet.

As I turned the tap (or faucet, for our American friends) on and washed off whatever that icky stuff was, I noticed an A4 laminated poster on the wall above the hand basin.

The title of the poster had the title *Hand Wash 12 Steps*, accompanied by a diagram advertising the twelve steps you should be taking to fully cleanse your hands.

I scanned through it, not quite heeding its message, and instead wondered who in the hell thought anyone needed this information.

One, turn on the tap with a paper towel. Two, rinse each hand thoroughly. Three, dispense and cover entire hand in soap. The entire hand? Are you mad?

Four, scrub palms thoroughly; use thumb in a circular motion on palm. Five, repeat, switching hands. Six, cover one hand over the other and scrub thoroughly. Seven, repeat, switching hands. Eight, rinse both hands. Nine, shake excess water carefully into the basin. Ten, dry hands with paper towel. Eleven, use paper towel to turn off tap. Twelve, dispose of towel and your hands are clean!

I stood there catatonic. Whatever next? 'Thirteen, open the door with your shirt sleeve in case some Neanderthal hasn't followed steps one through twelve?' Had Mr Bland been put in charge of toilet cleanliness, as well? I daren't peek inside the cubicle to see if a similar poster was hanging above the cistern. Bah, humbug.

My hands now thoroughly 'cleansed' (I couldn't resist, I followed steps one through nine to the tee), I looked around for that single-use paper towel that the guidelines had helpfully insisted that I use. There weren't any. But there was a hand drier on the wall.

I pressed the button. It wasn't working. We could've used this example for period one.

I knocked politely on Rachel's classroom door and slowly pushed it open. Rachel was in mid-teach. Around twenty-five sets of eyeballs belonging to fifteen year-old faces turned unanimously to me.

'Hi, Miss Weir. May I?' I hushed, indicating the back of the classroom.

'Yes Miss,' Rachel said, as she continued to teach. I reached the chair at the back on the corner. It was the same one Walter had been sitting in while he filled out his lines just before lunchtime.

'Okay,' Rachel returned to the class. 'Can anyone else give me an example, based on the scenario I've given you?' The kids scanned their notes. A couple of the students did not, though. Instead, they gazed at the window. This time, however, most of the other kids seemed to be taking part.

On the white board, Rachel had written the term "Price Penetration" and drawn an outline sketch of what looked like a hamburger underneath it. Either that, or a tampon.

'Yes, Carly,' Rachel said. 'What price point would you set?'

'If it was two days after the launch, and the break-even for it was £2.50, I'd reduce the price from £9.99 to maybe a fiver.

'And how long would you hold that reduction for, based on the target customer and one store location?' Rachel asked.

'Maybe two weeks to allow for the social media and in-store advertising campaign to kick in?'

'Very good,' Rachel said, writing Carly's answer on the board.

'Oh I get it now, Miss.' said a confident voice in the back row. 'So, you lower the price at launch.'

'Yes, and why do you do that, Oliver?'

'So you can convince people to try your new product.' Oliver said.

'That's right', Rachel added. 'We all know how we feel when there's a new product on the market. We're all like 'Nah, too expensive, I might not like it', and so companies drastically lower their price to entice people to buy it.'

'Yeah, that's happened to me before. My mum bought a new brand of washing powder that way,' Oliver said.

'What, your mum washes your clothes?' said a chubby kid next to him. 'You saying I smell, you fat squid?' Oliver retorted, before tutting to himself. 'Fat boy.'

'Oliver!' Rachel exclaimed, 'come on, you're better than that. Don't stoop to his level!'

'But, Miss, he dissed my mum.' Oliver pleaded.

'Yeah, at least I don't smell, though,' said the boy beside him.

'Fred,' Rachel said. 'Stop it, okay?'

'Why are people called Fred always fat, Miss?' Oliver said, defiantly. 'At least I can wash and change my clothes. You'll always be a chunky monkey.'

Okay, I have to hand it to this Oliver character - that was a good comeback. The rest of the class thought so, too, as it took them a good thirty seconds to stop laughing so that Rachel could continue.

'Miss,' came a female voice, 'why is it called price penetration?'

Again, more immature giggling. Penetration. Ho-ho.

'Okay, okay, grow up,' Rachel said. 'Think about it. What does the verb 'penetrate' actually mean? I was going to ask where you'd seen it used before, but I think it's better to avoid that.' Rachel smiled as the class chuckled.

'Shouldn't it be called 'Price Enticement', or something like that, Miss?' said another voice. A perfectly valid point.

'That's a very good point, well done. I think that's actually more accurate,' Rachel said. 'When it comes up in the exam next week - and it will, by the way - think of it like this.' Rachel drew a long, double-line curvature with a bell-shaped end. Oh my God, I thought to myself. That looked incredibly like a penis! The kids' chuckling indicated that they and I think alike. I think we were all a bit shocked. Rachel wasn't that naive, surely? Kids usually draw cocks on the board, but teachers rarely do. She must have a plan up her coffee-stained sleeve, right?

'Okay, so this is a penis, right? And this,' Rachel said, as she drew a fuzzy circle above it, 'is the vagina.'

Okay, where was this going? I felt the question being beamed into my head by the students in the class.

'The penis is the product, okay,' Rachel continued. 'Rigid and reliable, and up for some action. Eager to please, and up to the task,' Rachel said as she tapped the fuzzy circle with her pen.

'And this is the vagina, or the customer,' Rachel continued.

'Is that because they're all cunts, Miss?' Oliver asked to a deafening onslaught of surprised, choked-filled laughs.

'Oliver!' Rachel snapped, 'Right, I want to see you after class.'

'Sorry, Miss. Couldn't resist.'

Oliver nodded, accepting the challenge. Rachel returned to the board. 'So the vagina is, everyone, is their desire for the product. Now. How do we get the penis… into the vagina?'

'Penetration!' shouted the students in unison.

'That's correct! We take the penis,' Rachel said, circling her finger and thumb on one hand, and extended the forefinger on the other, 'and we insert it deep inside.' Rachel began penetrating her index finger into her makeshift hand-hole.

The kids chuckled, somewhat stupefied, by what they were witnessing. Rachel sped up the penetrating action.

'But once isn't enough. Through advertising and repeated pounding into the customer, we need them to part with their cash. In other words,' Rachel said viciously, as she went to town with her physical analogy, 'we gotta keep on going and going, never give up. Until - Bingo! They bite, and we get a sale. Or in this case, an orgasm.'

The children leaned back in their chairs. From my point of view, it seemed as if the analogy had not only worked, but proved to be one they wouldn't soon be forgetting in a hurry.

'Miss,' Oliver said. 'You're talking about the front hole right?'

'Yes, the vagina is generally considered to be the front hole,' Rachel smirked. 'Don't book the Comedy Store just yet, Oliver.'

Oliver smiled and accepted Rachel's retort. I think the Comedy Store reference was lost on most of the kids.

'Actually, you can do this with the back hole, but we'll

save the that one for when we talk about the banks.' The children laughed, although I'm not sure it was because they understood the concept of unrelenting and aggressive sodomisation of customers by the banks.

The School bell went off, and the children stepped out of their seats and packed up their papers and stationery. 'Remember guys, complete the Google Form I sent to you. I want it done by 7pm tonight.'

3:21pm. The kids shuffled out slowly from the class. For them, it was home time. 'Thanks for the lesson today, Miss.' Carly said as she walked past Rachel.

'You're welcome, sweetie,' Rachel replied, cleaning the white board. Last in line to leave was Oliver, with his bag over his shoulder.

'Oliver,' Rachel quipped, 'can I have a quick word, please?'

'Okay,' Oliver said, making his way over to Rachel.

'That altercation with Fred just there. What was that about?'

'Sorry, Miss.'

'Why did you call him fat?'

'He said my mum didn't wash my clothes.'

'No,' Rachel said. 'That's not what I asked. Why did you call him fat?'

'Dunno Miss.'

Rachel looked at him disappointedly. 'You're a smart guy, Oliver. One of the smartest in the class. Surely you should know better than that?' Oliver shuffled in his shoes, acknowledging her disappointment. He knew he'd acted immaturely.

'Don't attack people's size, Oliver,' Rachel said. 'Attack their character instead.'

Oliver's face lit up. 'What, Miss?'

'Attack their character. Something that they can't change. Like their personality, or something that they could never changed,' Rachel said, nonchalantly. 'Fred could lose weight one day. What will you do then when you want to attack him?'

Oliver literally had no words. Neither did I. This was callous stuff.

'You could have attacked his poor eyesight, or maybe the fact that he says "erm" like a cretin every other sentence.'

'Yes, Miss,' Oliver said, a smile creeping across his face. Was this a genuine teacher-student bond I saw solidifying before my very eyes?

'Don't you ever let me catch you taking the easy way out and attacking someone's physical appearance. You're better than that.'

'Yes, Miss.' Oliver said, trying to contain his smile. 'Thank you, you're the best.'

'I know,' Rachel smiled. 'Now, piss off.'

Oliver chuckled and left the room, happy.

I approached Rachel. 'Went well?'

'Sure.' Rachel threw the cleaning cloth onto the desk. 'Right, let's get out of here before someone spots us. It's home time!' Rachel said, trying not to yawn.

Just then, Gemma peeked her head around the door. 'Ten minutes till the training session, Raych. Thought I'd remind you.'

Rachel closed her eyes. 'Ohh, for fuck's sake.'

Two minutes later and Rachel and I were in her "main office" for the fourth (or was it fifth?) time today. She puffed on her cigarette quickly, trying to ingest as much nicotine as humanly possible. 'One more hour. Please go quick, I'm so tired.' Rachel blinked rapidly, the sunlight bouncing off her bleary eyes.

'How many do you smoke per day?'

'Maybe two. Give or take.'

'No way! You've had at least ten already today.'

'No, two packs,' she said, as she tossed the lit end into the bushes and replaced it with another. 'If I'm having a good day, one. If it's a bad day, God knows.'

She tossed the next cigarette into her mouth and lit the end of it with her lighter.

'I haven't even had a cup of coffee. I dunno how I've survived.' Rachel said, clicking the tip of the ash to the floor.

There was an elephant in the woods, and we both knew it. I decided to not so much broach the subject as bazooka it.

'Why did you hand in your notice?'

Rachel screwed her face and thought about the question. I say "thought" - I knew Rachel well enough to know that she had an answer for everything almost immediately. I also know that one doesn't just resign on a whim. She must have had her reasons.

'You ever feel like time is just running out, Joy?'

What, you mean like time goes too quickly?'

'No. Never mind.'

'Nah, tell me. Go on.'

'Everything here is a countdown. You must have noticed that, surely.'

'Countdown?'

'Yeah. Like Josie said earlier "Ooh, only four more days till half term!"'

'Yes' I said, puzzled as to her point. 'Isn't that a good thing?'

'What, half term? Or counting down?'

Hmm. I'd never thought of it like that. Sure, a well-deserved break is always a good thing. But she's making a precise point about the countdown. Rachel took another drag from her cigarette and exhaled dramatically, as seems to be the wont for most teachers.

'Every day someone says "Oh, only twenty more days till..." or "I can't wait for Saturday..." - is this what life is? A perpetual state of counting down till we're not working anymore?'

I admit, it was a good question to pose.

'I can't spend the rest of my life counting down, Joy,' Rachel continued. 'The time zips by so fast as it is. No sooner do we start a term than it ends. Life flashes right by. I can deal with the screaming and the meaningless educational jargon. I can deal with the boring bastards and the even more tedious dolts who make teaching their life. But I can't deal with the counting down, the wishing to speed up the days and living in abject misery until the next holiday. I can't do it.' Rachel sniffed. 'I'd rather do something more fulfilling.'

'Such as?'

'This teaching nonsense,' Rachel ignored me, 'half of them don't want to learn, and the other half who do are capable of learning by themselves. There are so many different ways of learning stuff. Take Business, for example. I learnt it all from *YouTube* and *Google* the night before I taught it. If the good ones are anything like me then they can do the same.'

Rachel expediently replaced her spent cigarette with another. 'Actually, I suspect the really good ones like Archie and Oliver probably do that anyway. So, what's the point of me if I'm inconsequential to the shit ones, and inconsequential to the good ones?'

'What about the kids in the middle?'

Rachel was taken aback by that question and thought it over as she took a drag from her *third* cigarette.

'Fuck it,' Rachel said flippantly, looking up at the sky.

When I first met Rachel this morning she was unwell but a confident force of nature. Now, some seven hours later, she's a completely changed person. The change was so drastic that I'd started to wonder if she wasn't really like this all along.

'"Fuck it?" Really?!' She was starting to anger me. The Rachel from this morning was vanishing before my eyes. She wasn't apologetic, though. As a matter of fact, she didn't even look at me. Who was I to interfere in her life any more than I had done already today?

At that moment, Rachel's phone beeped. She reached into her pocket and took it out.

'You mentioned you'd rather do something more "fulfilling"?'

'Yes.'

'What is that?'

'I'm going to be a writer.' Rachel closed her eyes and breathed in, slowly. The twittering of birds danced around us and a light breeze flew through the crevice of trees we were standing beside. Rachel stood there, enjoying it and smiled.

'You hear that?'

'No?'

'Exactly,' Rachel slurred, 'it's magical.'

Rachel breathed in and out with her eyes closed. I looked at the ground and kicked the dirt off my shoe. There were cigarettes everywhere. We were standing in an absolute ashtray! I lifted up my shoe and inspected the sole. A cigarette end butt had stuck to it. I managed to ping it to the ground with a flick of my finger.

I looked up at Rachel. She was making a snoring type of noise. Her hand at her side, with the end of her cigarette burning. Then, she began snoring for real. Here she was - a grown adult - fast asleep as she stood upright without any support. I'd never seen anyone do this before. I was fascinated.

I stepped forward to see if she was kidding. I waved my hand right in front of her snoring face. She wavered ever-so slightly, but was genuinely fast asleep. But it wasn't to last very long.

Beep-Beep! A text message.

Rachel awoke in shock and stumbled backwards. She scrambled for her phone in her pocket. As she looked at the screen, her face fell in the way faces fall when people learn that the result is malignant and cannot be operated on.

'Aww for fuck's sake,' Rachel said, before I had a

chance to ask what it was. 'It's Gemma. David's circle-jerk, forward-slash thought-shower session has just started. He's asking where I am. That's all I need,' Rachel groaned as she crushed the cigarette butt under her shoe, 'another excuse for the boring prick to have a "professional conversation" with me.'

13
A.R.S.E
Acronyms Really
Stifle Education

Rachel and I sprinted across the playground in tandem, late for class. We must have looked like a pair of guilty little schoolgirls running as fast as we could to avoid getting into too much trouble from the teacher. Sure enough, like a pair of guilty juveniles, we arrived at the bottom of the English department staircase. We caught our breath as I thought of potential excuses.

'Nah, no excuses,' Rachel said, catching her breath. 'God, I have to quit the fags.'

'Won't David be angry at you being late?'

'Yes. *The 'tard* sure hates tardiness,' Rachel joked as we began to ascend the stairs. 'Don't touch the rails, by the way. Never after lunchtime.'

'Thanks for the tip.'

We approached the training room slowly, virtually tiptoeing. As we stepped closer, we could hear David's monotonous tones draining the life out of whomever was listening to him in the room. Rachel pushed her way forward in front of me and stopped as we reached the door. We were just about out of view.

'Shit, he's started,' Rachel whispered, 'okay, here's the plan. We just walk in and sit down and say nothing, as if we're not late. All right?'

I nodded, rapidly, indicating my approval. Rachel adjusted her shirt collar and sniffed at her hands.

'Do I stink of fags?'

'Yes. Pretty badly.'

Rachel cleared her throat, held her head up high and confidently strode into the training room. I timidly followed behind her.

As I followed Rachel with a perma-apologetic look on my face, I quickly glanced around the room.

There were five pod-like desks arranged in the middle of the room, each with four or five teachers. Each pod had large flip chart paper on it, accompanied by a box of felt pens. The teachers all looked at us as we walked in, and not too many of them smiled.

I recognised Jeremy from the Comms Department at lunch. Mr Fiddle and Josie from science. I smiled at him. Instead of smiling back, they all pretended not to have seen me and looked down, suddenly fascinated by their own shoes.

Rachel found two available chairs on the pod farthest away from the front of the room, where David was waiting. The projector screen displayed a slide show with a cartoon illustration of a question mark.

Rachel and I hastily took our seats. 'Thank you Rachel and friend for joining us. Was there a better party on somewhere else?' Rachel smirked and adjusted her trousers, rattling in her seat. I simply looked down, coyly.

'As I was saying before the interruption, everyone,' David said, 'the rumours are not true. The National Association of Primary Education are not going regional. Where did you hear that, Mr Fiddle?'

'I'd heard that they changed 'National' to 'Regional'?' Mr Fiddle said. He scratched his beard and tried not to laugh.

'But then N.A.P.E would have to change to—'

David was obviously very slow to catch on. Everyone giggled at the joke. Finally, he got the joke.

'I don't find that especially amusing, Mr Fiddle'.

'It was just a joke, David. Lighten up.'

'I wouldn't throw stones in glass houses, Mr Fiddle.'

'What do you mean by that?'

'You heard,' David quipped as he turned to his right and pressed a button on the keyboard of his laptop. Up popped a picture of a cloud with a pensive-looking man looking up at it. Mr Fiddle shuffled in his seat quite angrily.

The title above the image on the board read: 'Mr David Bland's 'Professional and Experiential Development Objective'. Copyright (C) Mr David Bland, Deputy Assistant Head Teacher and Head of P.I.P.E (Professional, Institutional & Personal Extension), Maxwell Gooder's Comprehensive School, Wiltshire, England, United Kingdom'.

It was like the closing credits of the dullest movie you'd ever seen. I was now convinced - as were most of the staff at the school - that David was a straight-up, bona-fide bore.

'As you know, my recent brainchild initiative, The Professional and Experiential Development Objective had to be paused after school on Friday, due to a last-minute oversight discovered during the printing at reprographics.' David extended his pointing stick toward the screen.

Rachel leaned in to my ear. 'Do you see why they had to pause it, Joy?' Rachel giggled to herself, as she leaned back into her chair.

'Nevertheless, it is the essence of the initiative that the school wishes to exploit and deliver as of the next academic year. 'What is it', I hear you ask…'

No-one in the room looked as if they had ever asked this particular question. Ever.

'Well,' David droned on, 'quite simply, it's a series of after-school sessions designed to look at aspects of your

CPD, and further enhance them. The school has been allocated funding for exactly this purpose.' I turned to Rachel.

'What's CPD?'

'Continuing Professional Development' she mouthed back. I sit back in my chair, perhaps less the wiser for having asked.

'David,' Jeremy said, 'can I ask, why we have to have our mandatory CPD interfered with by your PAEDO? We're all a bit trained out to be honest.' A chorus of approval - and knowing chuckles - filled the room.

'Yea-huh sure. Look, Mr Sassoon, this isn't me, it's come from above.'

'But bringing this unwanted PAEDO into our school was your idea, wasn't it?' Josie asked, as she chewed on her pen.

'Yes, yes, it is, but—'

'And so you have the power to at least prevent the PAEDO from entering the school, don't you?' said another voice, fully aware of the insane offence it was causing David.

'Look, I'm afraid we're doing it.' David snapped, clearly offended that the others weren't as on board as he'd have hoped.

'If you had your way, David, you'd have PAEDOs in every school in the country, wouldn't you?' said a smirking Mr Fiddle, to a chorus of childish smirks. 'Would you say you're something of a paedo-phile yourself, David?'

'STOP SAYING THAT WORD! David blasted, losing his shit. The room dropped its jaw in utter shock.

'Shut up! Shut up! Shut up! Okay?!'

The room snapped to silence almost as fast as David's ignominy climbed out of his body, took human form, and proceeded to perform fellatio on itself.

'Har-har, very funny! Laugh at the funny offensive name! I'll report all of you to Mr Martelle for insubordination!' David yelped, deliriously. He adjusted his tie and breathed out, slowly, calming down. He looked like a bullied school kid trying to fight back.

'Now, can we have a training session, please?' David threatened.

Everyone nodded at David's request, presumably fearing for their jobs. That, and it was already fast approaching 3:50pm, and it was - as the classic teacher phrase goes - "their own time that they were wasting."

I turned to Rachel, expecting her to be elated. Instead, she had fallen asleep in her chair and missed all the hilarity.

'Clearly,' David bored forth, 'my Professional and Experiential Development Objective needs to be renamed. So, seeing as you're all so bloody creative, in your groups at your tables, I want you to draw up a list of all the areas of teaching development you think you'd like to have from September. Next academic next year. I'll give you ten minutes. Off you go.'

'Psst! Rachel wake up,' said the man at our table. He kicked her leg underneath it, jolting her awake.

'Eh! What happened?'

Rachel rubbed her eyes and looked around. Then she remembered where she was and became very depressed. She yawned and stretched her arms up into the air.

'Ugh. An hour of this. Fucking flip chart paper. Joy, listen, rule number one for training sessions. If you see flip chart paper, run!' she said. 'Right, what are we doing?'

I turned to the two other people at our table I hadn't yet met. 'Hey Robert, Isabelle. This is Joy. Joy, Robert and Isabelle,' Rachel said.

'Hi Robert. Isabelle.'

'Hello,' both said back to me.

'D'you know,' Isabelle said to the table,' David's PAEDO was quietly ushered into the school via the back door by SMT. He's done quite well with it.' Rachel squirmed in her seat.

'Yeah, he's just sucking up to SMT because he wants

Martelle's job in two year's time.'

Robert looked at Rachel and smiled. 'Yeah,' he said. 'Ugh, I can't be arsed with this. What do we have to write again?' He removed the lid from one of the felt pens with his teeth.

'Just make up any old shit. Write some teacher-ish words down. Do a Barnum on it.'

'Okay.' Robert wrote down the following words; Students, paperwork, marking, delivery and time-keeping.

'Brilliant, good work,' Rachel said. 'You thought of all those all on your own.'

'Yeah, they seem vague enough. I think I can bullshit this one.' Robert said, placing the pen on the desk.

Just then, David appeared and squatted down at our table, taking an interest in what Robert had written on the flip chart paper. He read the scribblings with a keen interest.

"Mmm. Yea-huh sure. Good. So, this first one, "Students"?'

'Yeah,' Robert snapped. 'We were thinking maybe we could have training with the students themselves,' Robert said, rattling off a sentence that was clearly being formed as it was said. 'Maybe in terms of their approach to their studies.'

'Wow', I thought. That made perfect sense, even to me. It actually sounded like a good answer. I think?

'Yea-huh sure, that's really great, Robert,' David added. 'I wonder, though, could we develop this thinking a bit further?'

'How d'you mean?' Isabelle asked.

'Well, you say here that you would like to know what students are thinking. How could you do that? I'll leave you guys to have a think about that for two minutes,' said David, patronisingly knocking the tabletop as a sign of goodwill, before moving off to ensure the next table wanted to commit suicide due to his presence.

'Oh God, I just want to go home,' Rachel said, closing

her eyes in exasperation.

'Nah mate,' Robert said. 'Year eight parents evening tonight.'

Rachel playfully slammed her head to the table as a response. 'Kill me now.' She lifted her head back up, her stressed dark brown hair messily covering her face. Isabelle and Robert chuckled.

David left the neighbouring desk and returned to the front. 'Okay everyone,' he said, clapping his hands. 'Can I have your attention, please.'

Everyone stopped chattering. His Lordship had spoken. They all looked at him. 'Some really encouraging ideas from each of the tables there. Miriam, can I ask you what your table came up with, as I think it exemplifies what we're after?'

Miriam, clearly in her twenties, stood up.

'Well, we were discussing about behavioural issues, and how we can set the right atmosphere for the class. We'd like more sessions on that.' David smiled and nodded his head. The more culturally-astute person may even have read it as somewhat demeaning.

'Yea-huh sure, Miriam. That's excellent, thank you. Okay, so we have a few good ideas, here. I wonder, could we blue-sky this one and maybe come up with some suitable initials, or maybe acronyms, for some of the ideas you've had.'

Rachel put up her hand, seeming to deliberately cause trouble, judging by the inexpedient look on her face. 'Yes, Rachel?'

'Don't we have enough acronyms already, David? I mean, come on!' Rachel said, to a sea of surprised faces. "She didn't, did she?!"

'Too many acronyms?' David enquired, feigning befuddlement.

'Yes. I mean we've all got our ILPs in order, and SMT know our MO when it comes to our PPs and recordings on E-JIT. But frankly the SOWs take a long time to create, and it's all a bit 'FML' - as the FML department will tell you - when CPD sessions like this and your PAEDO get in the way of our work, FFS. I mean, WTF, David?'

David stood back, shocked. He was genuinely unable to process this request. But Rachel didn't stop there.

'David, I'm sure all your wonderful cloud-shaped initiatives and aircraft-based thinking sounds good in your head. But I think I'm just a bit fed up with all of it.'

'Don't hold back, Rachel. Tell us how you really feel.' David said, folding his arms.

'Just speak proper English,' Rachel replied. 'And why do you keep telling us to "blue sky this one" and "think outside of the box" all the time?'

'No, I simply want us to think beyond our—'

'Beyond our what? Capabilities?'

'No, it's just that I—'

'That you've swallowed an entire teaching manual and can't communicate with us on a human level? What are you, a robot?'

'Rachel,' David offered, 'I think you're taking this all wrong.'

'I really don't, David,' Rachel continued. 'To tell us to think outside of the box is to imply that until this point we never had done at all. Right?' Rachel looked to the other teachers in the room. 'Am I right, guys?'

Not a peep.

'When we're preparing classes, when we're faced with a difficult situation, we'd be dead if we didn't think creatively. Look, David, that stupid picture behind you,' Rachel said, as everyone's attention veered toward the picture of the man thinking. '"Blue sky thinking"? What does that even mean? Tell me, I'm all ears.'

'Well, it means thinking outside the box.'

'You don't know what you're talking about, do you?'

David closed his mouth. He can't worm his way out of this one. Watching him, I began to take pity. Despite its comic potential in word form, in actuality, it was really, really sad to watch.

'Does anyone here actually know what it means?' Rachel posed, awaiting a response. Robert and Isabelle froze. The other teachers either didn't know, or were genuinely afraid to say anything. It's tempting to say Rachel was having her William Holden moment. I'm not precisely sure just how mad she was, but I could definitely tell she was on the verge of not taking it anymore.

'Oh, forget it,' Rachel said. 'I'm obviously alone.'

Rachel slumped into her chair and folded her arms. Robert shot her a look; "are you mad?!" David adjusted his tie.

'Happy now?'

'Yeah.'

'Okay. Good. So, as I was saying, I'd like you all to come up with an acronym for our particular area of development. This can be done either outside or - as Rachel prefers – "inside the box".' Everyone at each table started chattering among themselves, beginning the task at hand.

Ordinarily most of the teachers would have been making their way home about now. But here they were, exercising their grey matter in a way that promised to extend their professional career. Most of their faces, however, were strained; revealing their suffrage of time seeming to move slower.

Rachel, on the other hand, had made herself at home by placing her feet on the table and eating two sticks of chewing gum.

She fiddled aimlessly with her biro between her fingers in a world of her own. Robert and Isabelle seemed to be struggling with the task at hand and so, like most teachers in their situation, had given up and started talking about personal stuff.

'Only four more days till half term,' Isabelle sighed.

Rachel hung her head to the side and snorted in defiance. 'Ughhh! Someone get me out of here!'

'Yep, and forty-something till summer holidays!' Robert replied.

'Got anything planned for next week?'

'Not much,' Isabelle quipped. 'Probably spend the first three days marking those A2 practice exam papers. I was thinking about visiting my niece in Bristol on Friday.'

'Nice, nice.' Robert nodded.

Rachel chewed her gum harder and rolled her eyes. Isabelle smiled at her. 'How about you Rachel? Any plans?' Rachel snorted and rested her hands on her stomach as she leaned back in her chair.

'Oh yes,' Rachel insisted. 'Major plans. And none of them involve this dump.'

'Okay guys, five more minutes!' David threatened from the other side of the room. The pace of the other participants picked up, just as our table's was grinding to a halt.

Robert turned to me. 'So, Joy, you're a journalist? How's Rachel been today?' I smiled and chuckled.

'Yes, she's great.' Robert nudged Isabelle and winked at me. 'You picked a real star to follow, there, mate.'

'Fuck off, Bob,' Rachel said, with a cheeky grin as she shooed his leg under the table.

'Yeah, Rachel's terrific,' Robert continued, 'the kids love her, she gets good grades. She'll be head teacher in five years, no sweat.' Rachel rolled her eyes once again and blew a small bubble with her chewing gum.

'So, Joy,' Isabelle asked. 'How are you getting on with the kids?'

'Oh, they're great!' I replied with a smile. 'We seem to be getting along just fine.'

'And how are you finding fingering them?'

'I beg your pardon?!'

'*Fingeringham*. Have you managed to visit the town centre, yet?'

'Oh, I see. No, not yet. I'm not staying long enough. I've got to get back and start writing the book.'

'Oh, yes, this famous book. Have you written anything that I might have seen or read?'

I hate this question, mainly because this book is my first foray into the profession. Prior to this I worked in retail, and managed to climb up to management level in a clothing store. You may have heard of the store. It had three words in its name, the first of which was "British" and the third was "Stores". I'm not sure where I stand legally on naming the chain, so please forgive my coy, if not wholly blatant circumvention of its name.

The closure of the company meant I quickly had to find replacement work, but the economy had been devastated in the UK, so I decided to take my chances with journalism. I'd always been told I had good people and analytical skills, so this seemed like a natural fit for me. Well, all except the actual writing part of it.

'No, this is my first story, actually. But I plan to do a whole series, maybe two or three every year.'

Rachel smiled and looked at me, for maybe the first time since lunch. She smiled and revealed her chewing gum. 'Joy's awesome. A real inspiration,' she said. 'Maybe one day we'll be rivals in the literary world, eh?'

I blushed, not knowing how to react.

'Okay everyone,' David shouted from the back of the room. 'Two more minutes.'

Rachel swiped her feet off the tabletop and pulled herself forward, in a seemingly quick change of pace.

'Right,' Rachel barked, nodding at David's pen. 'Let's get this tedious nightmare over with. Gimme the pen.'

Three minutes later, and I was feeling extremely nervous. Robert and Isabelle were, as well. Rachel dominated the activity, and wrote things on our table's flip chart paper. We knew what she'd done. We also knew that she had stubbornness to actually go through with presenting her work to the rest of the class.

'Okay. Time's up, everyone. Pens down, please,' David announced, as he returned to the front of the room. 'Okay, who'd like to go first?'

Rachel immediately threw her hand up in the air like an overzealous child. Another teacher in a team of four at the front of the room also put up her hand.

No prizes for guessing who David chose to ignore first. 'Yes, Ellie,' David said to the teacher who put her hand up second. 'Your group can go first!'

Ellie, a petite girl with an androgynous air about her, stood up and smiled. 'Well, our table were discussing the benefits of kinaesthetic activities in the classroom, and so we wanted to explore the idea of using more of it in practice.'

David beamed in the way that normal people do when a loved one reveals they're going to have a baby. 'So we came up with 'Variety'; because kids enjoy a varied classroom experience. 'Yields'; because enjoyment begets an appetite for knowledge. 'Kinaesthetic'; as in hands-on learning, and finally 'Education'; as it brings the whole process full circle. It spells VYKE.'

Ellie lifted up her flip chart paper, with VYKE written in big, bold red felt tip pen.

David smiled as a polite round of applause filled the room. 'Thank you, everyone,' Ellie said, pleased with herself as she took her seat.

'DYKE, more like' Rachel muttered to herself, annoyed.

'Yea-huh sure,' David quipped. 'Very good. Very well done to the P.E. department.'

Ellie sneered at David. She seemed to take offence at his plaudit. 'What are you trying to say?'

David pleaded, realising his remark had been taken the wrong way. 'No, no. I meant nothing by it, I assure you—'

'—you're saying we're all thick in P.E. aren't you?' Ellie continued, angrily.

'No-no, I assure you I—' tried David, unsuccessfully.

'Don't think we don't know what people say about us.'

'Look, Ellie - and the whole department - I assure you that is not the case,' David grovelled. 'We've nothing but the utmost respect for the contribution you make to the school.' Ellie folded her arms and sighed, not believing a word. Rachel spotted her opportunity to throw her hand in the air, indicating that she wanted to be picked next. 'Okay,' David said. 'Who's next?'

Rachel strained her outstretched arm in the air and made a fist with her hand. David avoided looking at it as he went around the room. She opened her first and held up her middle finger at him and waved it around. David was saved from having to choose Rachel when, seconds later, another hand lifted slowly into the air.

'Ah, yes. Elijah, our wonderful NQT,' David smiled, somewhat relieved. 'The History Department!'

'So, on our table we discussed the importance of homework,' Elijah explained in his weak Irish accent. 'It's important that we get kids working at home, hopefully with the help of their parents, and we know this can be a challenge.'

'Yea-huh sure, Elijah. A very promising point.'

'Yeah,' Elijah continued, 'so we came up with a simple initiative. "Homework Includes Thought, Research And Theoretical, Evaluative Summaries", which spells out a phrase we hope to see increase, if the initiative works,' said Elijah, as he produced the flip chart paper. 'HIT RATES is the name, and we're hoping to 'up' ours.'

Once again, another round of polite applause. The look of nerves and anxiety from the as-yet unselected tables was palpable. Not that you'd expect such behaviour from teachers, but clearly a lot of pride and professional clout was being held to account in this room, judging by the participants' faces. A number of these teachers were patently potential David-Blands-in-the-Making. Rachel smirked to herself, and quickly scribbled some words down on the flip chart paper.

'Yea-huh, sure. Excellent!' David exclaimed. 'What I like about it is that it's easy to remember, which is beneficial to the students, and also contains some of the more essential elements of producing exemplary work. HIT RATES. Very well done.'

'Thank you,' Elijah said, 'we're thinking of using it next from September.' David nodded, eyes closed, as if his revering, obedient novice had finally mastered the art of pedagogical combat.

'Yes, it's great,' Rachel barked, prompting everyone's attention to turn her way. 'But aren't you better off rearranging the words?'

David screwed his face, puzzled. 'What do you mean, Rachel?'

'Well I was thinking you could reorder it, and let the students figure out the correct term. Maybe pose it as a puzzle,' Rachel offered.

David nodded agreeably - he's not totally hating this idea. 'How would that work, exactly?'

'You scramble the words. Like this; Research, And, Thought, Summaries, Homework,' Rachel said, reading from her own flip chart paper.

'Includes, Theoretical and Evaluative. Or something like that. Present that to the students, and see if they can rearrange the words. We all know, if students take ownership of their learning and discover the answer for themselves, that they take it more seriously. They'd be more likely to actually enact HIT RATES'.

Ever-the-keen NQT Elijah quickly scribbled down the suggestion on the corner of his flip chart paper.

Everyone in the room nodded at Rachel, impressed. This was a stellar idea. David smiled. Rachel had finally atoned for her attack on him ten minutes ago.

Even I smiled, thinking she was back on board. My pity for David started to dissipate somewhat. The atmosphere in the room started to get more comfortable. It almost began to be fun.

But one person wasn't smiling – Elijah - who finally managed to process Rachel's idea and arrive at a very worrying conclusion.

'But, Rachel,' Elijah said, examining his scribbling. 'That spells RAT SHITE.'

'Yes,' Rachel said, trying not to laugh. 'It does, doesn't it? And it perfectly sums up your group's stupid idea.'

Everyone except Elijah and David burst out laughing. One teacher nearly choked on his pen lid. Elijah sank back to his seat. Poor guy. Rachel had blatantly used him as her pawn in getting back at David.

'Sorry Elijah. No offence, but your effort is the result of trying too hard. You and I both know that phrase will never work with the kids. It's a stupid idea. Noble, sure, but also stupid. I admire your sincerity, though.'

I take back what I said about the atmosphere. The room was back to square one once again.

The smirking died down as David's facial reaction threatened the room, in that sort of closed-minded way we'd all become accustomed to by now from him.

'Yea-huh, sure. Okay Rachel, seeing as you're such the authority on this particular subject, why don't we hear what your group came up with?'

'Sure,' Rachel snapped, standing up from her chair. Robert held her back, scared.

'Rachel. Please don't,' Robert mouthed to her. 'They'll think Isabelle and I did it.'

'Don't worry, I'll take the credit for this one,' Rachel said, reassuringly. 'Okay guys. Well, my table and I were mostly discussing what we were going to be doing for the half term, and also for the summer. I'd say we spent maybe eighteen of the twenty minutes David gave us to do this task just pissing around,' Rachel said, matter-of-factly.

David's face was a picture. If in fact that picture was of a Nazi concentration camp guard who'd lost all interest in fascism and had decided he wanted to become a ballerina.

'So, here's what we came up with…'

14

The Kamikaze Teacher's Handbook

All eyes were on Rachel. She scanned our group's flip chart paper and then looked up and smiled.

'Firstly, as teachers, I'm sure we'd all agree that the information we have needs to be distributed to the children in our classes. We do this through encouraging them to acquire the information and consolidate their knowledge, usually by producing work as a test of their understanding,' Rachel said, as everyone listened intently. 'It's a bit like Bloom's Taxonomy, in that respect.'

She wasn't saying anything contentious, nor was she being deliberately flippant. She meant everything she was saying. 'Also, where would we be without active decision-making? We do this every day in our lives, and it's a skill we need to teach our children.'

David glared at Robert and nodded his head, proudly. Robert, and to a lesser extent, Isabelle, were not only relieved by what Rachel was saying, but also smiled back at David as if they had been instrumental in Rachel's answer. She smiled back down at them.

'But do we really do this? I mean, really? Most of what we do here is training the students to pass exams. I can't really speak for Josie in Science, or Ellie in Sports, or even

Jeremy in Comms. But, certainly in English, all we're doing is teaching to the exam,' Rachel said, starting to emote her true feelings. Most of the teachers in the room nodded and agreed. 'I can see from all your reactions that you feel the same way.'

'Hear, Hear!' said a voice from the back.

Rachel tried for a smile, but she was evidently stirring inside. She cleared her throat. Her voice began trembling for the first time today.

'What next, after the classroom? Do we stop learning? Do we leave school and say "Sod it, that's it. Stacking shelves in Tesco for me!" or "University it is!" and leave learning behind? No, never. So it's ultra important we make sure the kids - each and every one who walks through the front gate - leave here with the ability to learn.' Rachel said, fighting the urge to cry.

'They need to heighten their education, not the ability to just pass a test. We have enough suck-up "yes men", don't we, David?'

He looked back at her, and then around the room with a 'Who, me?' look on his face.

Rachel cleared her throat to try and stop her voice from wobbling too much. 'We need individuals who think for themselves. As I'm sure you've all noticed there's not a helluva lot of thinking going on at this school at the best of times'.

A few of the teachers chuckled, including David. He seemed genuinely moved by this speech. I have to admit that I did, too. For the first time today I felt genuinely proud of Rachel. She continued.

'Haven't the government - or any decision-maker that counts - ever heard the phrase "just because you keep weighing the pig it doesn't make it fatter"?'

Rachel took the flip chart paper into her hand, and stood up. She tapped me gently on the shoulder, and looked down at me. Her eyes were glazed with tears.

'And so, here's what we came up with,' said Rachel. She

opened up the flip chart paper, and everyone gasped! I looked at it. It said "DICKHEAD". Once again, Rachel cleared her throat and wiped her nose with her shirt sleeve.

'Distribute Information, Consolidate Knowledge, Heighten Education and Active Decisions,' Rachel said. David closed his eyes and shook his head. The others just sat there, stunned.

'Dickhead. We all believe in it, and we all know how important it is. Much like Steven's effort it, too, has a double meaning,' Rachel said, looking at David. 'It also perfectly describes Mr. Bland.'

'Hey, now hang on a minute, Rachel.' David protested. He wasn't angry. Quite the opposite, in fact. He began to show a human, compassionate side. Here was a woman whose life was changing in front of his very spectacles.

Rachel screwed up the flip chart paper in her hands and turned it into a ball of paper. A tear rolled down and off her cheek.

'I can't do this anymore,' Rachel blurted, seconds away from becoming very emotional. She tossed the screwed-up ball of flip chart paper to David. He instinctively reacted and caught it awkwardly in both hands.

'Are you quite finished, Rachel?' David asked, calmly.

Her bottom lip quivered violently, and another tear rolled down her cheek. Her hand was shaking as she wiped her face, and tried for a final, parting sentence.

'In more ways than you can imagine.'

Rachel quickly made for the door as she started crying. Everyone raised their eyebrows in stunned silence.

Rachel had nosedived her career in front of her peers. And there I was; this complete stranger, standing alone like a complete idiot. I raised a smile to the catatonic faces staring back at me.

'Well. I've had a wonderful day, and thank you so much for your kindness. Goodbye!'

I quickly made my escape.

Moments later we were in Rachel's classroom. She's hastily threw some belongings into her bag like a woman on cocaine, crying her teacher's eyes out. 'You got your things?'

I picked up my bag and slipped it over my shoulder. 'Yes,' I said, deeply concerned for her. She's bawling her eyes out, and just wants to escape the building.

I stepped toward her and placed my hands on the side of her shoulders. 'We're not leaving here till you've let it all out.'

Rachel sobbed harder and put her hands on me. She buried her soaking wet face on my shirt and cried into it in a way my dry cleaning service would never believe if I'd told them.

I stroked Rachel's hair as she cried. 'Hey, it's okay. Just let it out.'

We made our way down the stairs and across the playground. Rachel had stopped bawling like a little girl, but her face of course was a beetroot-red picture of post-turmoil.

Heading our way was a student, carrying a pair of trainers by its laces. It was Archie. He was looking very solemn and sorry for himself.

'Hi, Miss,' Archie said, softly. 'Have you been crying?

Rachel pathetically spat out a laugh as she sniffed. She wiped her face. 'No,' she lied, 'just think I'm coming down with someone,' she said, not realising her vocabulary error.

'You mean 'something', Miss?'

Rachel laughed. 'Yes. What are you still doing here, it's half past four?'

'Yeah, had an hour's detention. Just got out.'

Rachel squinted at Archie and wiped her nose with her sleeve. 'You? A school detention?' Rachel asked, indicating her surprise that such a wonderful person had been punished by the school. 'How did that happen?'

Archie smirked. You could tell from his visage that he

knew Rachel would be surprised. They clearly didn't have that kind of teacher-student relationship.

'Mr McDonnell in History. I hate him.'

'What did you do?'

'I called him a twat in front of the class.'

Rachel laughed, heartily 'That wasn't a very good move, was it?'

'Nope. But he's such a tosser. Why can't we have you for tutor, Miss?'

Rachel tilted her head and patted his shoulder. 'Aww, you're so sweet.'

His remark nearly started her off again. 'Look, Archie, you'll learn very soon that you have to work with people you don't like very much. But the best thing is to just chew it back, say nothing and get on with it.'

'Yeah. I know.'

'Good.'

Archie smiled. 'You're the best teacher. See you tomorrow,' he said as he continued on his path toward home.

Rachel wiped her cheek yet again, and snorted loudly. She quickly shook it off. 'Whatever.'

As we approached reception, the lack of human beings really rang through the walls. The receptionist was not at the window, and Mr Martelle was not in his office.

'Just put your name badge through the window, they'll pick it up later,' Rachel said to me. I slipped off the badge and looked at it. I had forgotten it said Mrs. Joyce Altwild. But then, barely anyone read it. I placed it on the counter and moved toward the door.

Just before we reached the exit, Rachel noticed something on the wall. 'Oh, that's not doing my OCD any good.'

She was looking at a picture. In fact, it was the picture that had caught my attention every time I found myself in reception. The Picasso thing. She unhooked it from the wall and analysed it. 'Hmm.' She span it around 180 degrees.

'C'est magnifique!' She placed it back on the wall. We both stepped back to look at it. I tilted my head slightly and squinted my eyes. 'You like that?' she asked me.

'Oh, I see now!' I'd finally figured it all out. 'It's The Eiffel Tower! That's the building, and those are the lights up the side in red, white and blue.'

'Je suis Maxwell Gooder.'

'Well, not for much longer?' I said, indicating her lunchtime antics.

'C'est vrai.'

I stared at the painting which now looked remarkably like a spluttering, upside-down neon vagina. 'Which student did that, then?'

'I did.' said Rachel, as she smiled and nodded at the door.

We emerged from the main building and into the glorious May sunshine. The first genuinely sizzling hot day of the year.

It had cooled down somewhat since the heat of the mid-morning sun, but it was still very warm. We hurried along the entrance grounds and into the small, tucked away car park. Our pace slowed as we approached Rachel's car.

'I bet you weren't expecting that to happen, huh?'

'Expecting what?

'You know. The whole "Kamikaze Teacher" episode.'

I must admit - no - I wasn't expecting any of that to have happened today. My first journalistic experience following someone in their profession and they quit their job on the day. I hope this isn't a recurring theme in my future book entries for the *In Their Shoes* series.

'No,' I said. 'That was a bit out of the blue!'

'Actually, that's quite a good name for my first book. Kamikaze. Maybe *The Kamikaze Teacher's Handbook*.'

'What will it be about?'

'It'll be a teacher manual, but, you know, like a proper no BS type-thing. All the stuff a teacher really needs to know, like some of the stuff I've shown you today. Not any of that stupid Bloom's Taxonomy rubbish.'

'What's Bloom's Taxidermy?' I asked, as Rachel threw a cigarette into her mouth.

'Don't worry,' she quipped. She sparked up her cigarette and pocketed her lighter. 'Life's too short for that!'

We eventually arrived at her car. This was it. We were parting ways, now. We may never see each other again.

'So, Rachel,' I said, trying to dispel the silence between us. 'Thanks so much for allowing me to spend the day with you. It's been very informative.'

'Oh, you're welcome,' Rachel said, as she pointed her car key at her Red Volvo. Bip-Bop. It unlocked. 'I've enjoyed it, too.' We reached her car and she opened the back passenger door. She threw her bag inside.

'Oh' I remembered, 'don't you have parents evening tonight?'

'Yeah. I think I'll skip it this time,' Rachel said. 'I'll only end up telling parents what they want to hear to avoid a confrontation anyway.'

Rachel closed the back passenger door with her knee, and wiped her eyes. 'Look, Joy, I'm sorry for the way I acted earlier.'

'Which bit?'

Rachel laughed, which made me smile. True enough. It had been a bit of a tumultuous day for us both.

'Ah, that bit where I got a antsy at you before lunch. I just, you know, didn't take it very well. I was wrong. You'd make an excellent teacher, you know.'

'You really think so?'

'Definitely.'

I was moved by that remark. Perhaps one day I might become a teacher. I love people generally, and I adore children. I used to relish the chance of spending time with them and teaching them new ideas and encouraging them to be the best people they could. I thought about it a lot when I was younger, before my own school executed my love for learning and turned me into the cynical and deceitful little brat I would become.

'Teaching's not for everyone. But you'd do well at it.' She opened the door of her car and climbed into the driver's seat. 'You *are* going to change my name for the book, right?'

I smiled. 'Yes, of course. Do you have a name in mind?' Rachel thought about it for a moment as she put her seatbelt on.

'Rachel. I always liked the name Rachel,' she said. 'Maybe Rachel Weir? Something like that?

'You got it. "Rachel",' I said with a cheeky grin.

Rachel turned on the ignition and the car spluttered to life. *Ironic* by Alanis Morissette blared out of the radio at an ungodly volume. She scrambled to turn it down. We both smiled.

'Now, that's irony, right?' laughed Rachel. We both stood there for a second as the song played. It acted as a quick summation of the day we'd had.

I looked at her with a great fondness. I'd spent the day with Rachel the teacher. But here presented to me is Rachel, a young woman with dreams and aspirations, who was about to start a new journey during the summer.

The song came to an end. It was replaced by something more lively. The opening violin melody was unmistakable.

'You don't think I've made a massive mistake, do you, Joy?' Rachel asked. Just then, the song's opening violins gave way to the beat kicking in.

'Well, as long you're ha—'

'—oh! I love this song,' Rachel interrupted, happily. 'You know it?'

'Yes, I love it too!'

'It's *Rather Be*, by Clean Bandit. Great song,' Rachel

said, nodding her head to the music. 'Right now, I'd rather be at home. In bed!' Rachel joked. Actually, she wasn't joking at all. Her misty eyes said everything. And seeing her mist up got me going, too. I get like this, sometimes. The good stuff always makes me go, and it can get embarrassing.

She started her engine and revved the accelerator. 'It's been fun, Joy.' She reversed out toward my car. 'A real Joy!' she laughed, and waved as she drove off and out of my life.

'Bye, Rachel!' I said, waving back.

It's fair to say that it's been something of a crazy day. I thought spending the day with a teacher in a common comprehensive school like Maxwell Gooder's would be straightforward; teaching, chatting and with mostly obedient children. I wasn't expecting the experience I had had at all. In a short space of time, I had learnt so much. As this is the first entry in the series, it makes me wonder if I've completely underestimated this new journalistic venture I've embarked on.

On the other hand, it is comforting to note that Rachel - much like the other teachers - evidently holds our children's future and lives close to her heart. While it may not always have been so explicit, Rachel does love those kids. The profession has clearly worn her down, though. Perhaps I had managed to draw out the devil in her. It made it difficult to see her caring and compassionate pastoral side.

I turned to go to my car. When I laid eyes on it, I stopped dead in my tracks. I was stunned. Shocked.

All my windows - including the windscreen - were smashed. Jesus Christ! What happened! I ran up to the bonnet of the car and noticed someone had key scratched it with messy zig zags. My two front tyres were slashed. Who could have done this!?

I looked left - the sports department. No-one. I looked

right. Trees. I spun around, looking for the culprit. Then, it dawned on me. This could have happened anytime between now and 8am this morning.

I took a step back and inspected the driver's side of my car. Ah, I think I know what's happened. There's been some confusion.

On the driver's side, someone had daubed 'Nonce Scumbag' and 'Sick Beast' in giant black letters across the entire length of my car. I checked the other side.

There's simply no way I could drive one hundred plus miles back home in this! I won't reveal what the other side said but it was much worse. The smashed particles of glass from the window were scattered over the driver's seat. They'd even pinched the packet of mints I had in the cup holder!

I took out my phone - I needed to call the rescue squad. The screen on my phone reminded me that there was no network available. I was trapped.

How the hell was I going to explain this to Jay?

Acknowledgements

For K

<u>Also to:</u>

My parents and brothers
Anyone who's ever taught for a living, this is for you
All the wonderful people on the 20booksto50k forum
All my wonderful beta readers - you know who you are
Sarah Benjamin who convinced me to go through with it
My previous colleagues in Further and Secondary Education
Fellow author Craig Martelle for all his support
and use of his name for the head teacher
Beth Strang and all the staff and students at Maxwell
Gooder's Comprehensive School, Fingeringham, Wiltshire, UK

And to all the naysayers and doubters,
wherever you may be…
I love you all.
And don't worry,
there's plenty more to come.

Joy Attwood returns in The Actor!

GET YOUR FREE E-BOOK!

Subscribe to the Chrome Valley Books website and get your free e-book! (PDF & Kindle)

In Their Shoes - 'One Size Fits All'

The hilarious prequel to the **In Their Shoes** *series!*

bit.ly/cvbsubs

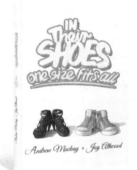

Continue the hilarity with In The Shoes – The Actor!

Available at Amazon.

Get your copy now!

About the author

Andrew Mackay is an author, screenwriter and film critic. A former teacher, Andrew has written dozens of feature-length screenplays and is writer/director of two films: The Scared of Death Society and The Making of Mutant Chronicles: A Documentary.

His passions include daydreaming, storytelling, smoking and caffeine (though not always in that order).

A word from the author

I hope you enjoyed this book! There's plenty more 'Joy' to come in the series as she continues her investigative journey!

If you enjoyed the book, please do leave a review online at Amazon. Reviews are integral for authors and I would dearly appreciate it.

I love to engage directly with my readers. Please get in touch with me - I look forward to hearing from you!

Email: andrew@chromevalleybooks.com
Facebook: facebook.com/chromevalleybooks
Twitter: @Andrew_CVB

And don't forget to subscribe to **chromevalleybooks.com** for my blog, giveaways, upcoming titles and free e-books!

Happy reading!

Made in the USA
Monee, IL
15 June 2020